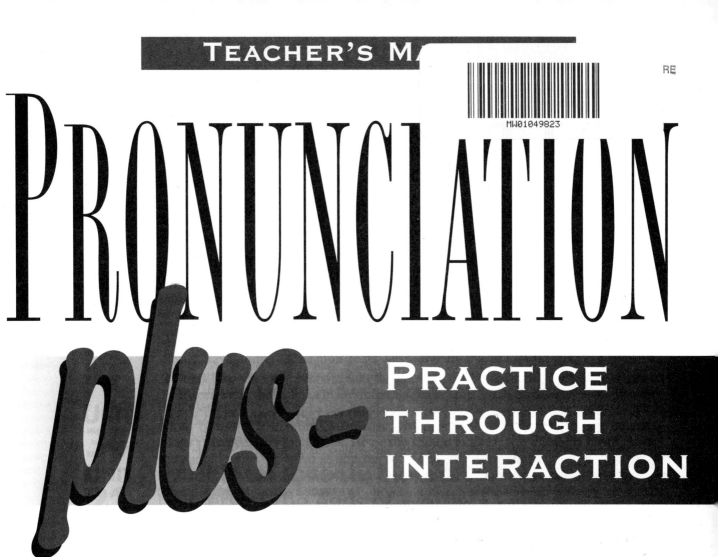

TEACHER'S M...

RE

MW01049823

PRONUNCIATION
plus—

PRACTICE
THROUGH
INTERACTION

MARTIN HEWINGS

SHARON GOLDSTEIN

NORTH AMERICAN ENGLISH

CAMBRIDGE
UNIVERSITY PRESS

0 571820

PUBLISHED BY THE PRESS SYNDICATE OF THE UNIVERSITY OF CAMBRIDGE
The Pitt Building, Trumpington Street, Cambridge CB2 1RP, United Kingdom

CAMBRIDGE UNIVERSITY PRESS
The Edinburgh Building, Cambridge CB2 2RU, United Kingdom
40 West 20th Street, New York, NY 10011–4211, USA
10 Stamford Road, Oakleigh, Melbourne 3166, Australia

First published 1999

Printed in the United States of America

Typeset in New Aster and Frutiger

A catalogue record for this book is available from the British Library

ISBN 0 521 57797 7 Student's Book
ISBN 0 521 57795 0 Cassettes
ISBN 0 521 57796 9 Teacher's Manual

Book design, page makeup, and text composition: Leon Bolognese & Associates

Contents

Key to phonetic symbols

Vowels		**Consonants**	
Symbol	**Examples**	**Symbols**	**Examples**
/ɑ/	stop, father	/b/	back, about
/æ/	apple, hat	/d/	dance, need
/aw/	out, town	/dʒ/	job, age
/ay/	ice, drive	/ð/	this, other
/ɛ/	end, red	/f/	four, off
/ey/	train, say	/g/	give, big
/ɪ/	if, big	/h/	hat, behind
/iy/	jeans, see	/k/	car, week
/ow/	phone, no	/l/	late, call
/ɔ/	call,* short	/l̩/	bottle, medal
/ɔy/	join, boy	/m/	make, lamp
/ʊ/	book, put	/n/	near, sun
/uw/	soon, too	/n̩/	button, garden
/ə/	up, cut, ago	/ŋ/	long, working
/ər/	word, first, answer	/p/	pay, keep
		/r/	rain, there
		/s/	same, nice
		/ʃ/	should, push
		/t/	talk, light
		/tʃ/	chair, watch
		/v/	very, live
		/w/	walk, swim
		/y/	yes, you
		/z/	zoo, easy
		/ʒ/	television, usual
		/θ/	thanks, bath

*Many Americans and Canadians say this word with the vowel /ɑ/.

To the teacher

Pronunciation Plus is a set of materials designed to help intermediate-level students improve their pronunciation of North American English. Many of the activities will also be of use to more advanced students. The materials can supplement any general ESL or EFL course or be used in a specialized course on pronunciation.

Content

The teaching of pronunciation has traditionally focused on individual sounds. Difficulties with English pronunciation, however, often involve several different features; for example, a single mispronounced word may be the result of incorrect word stress and confusion caused by spelling, as well as mispronounced sounds. *Pronunciation Plus* gives attention to a wide range of features that cause difficulty for speakers of other languages. Each of the eight parts of the book focuses on one of these areas: (1) vowel sounds, (2) consonant sounds, (3) consonant clusters, (4) word stress and rhythm, (5) changes that take place in conversational speech, (6) intonation, (7) the pronunciation of common grammatical items, and (8) the connection between spelling and pronunciation. The Introduction in the Student's Book teaches ways of asking about and checking pronunciation.

Because the different aspects of pronunciation are interrelated and problems with pronunciation often involve more than one feature, some features are reintroduced and practiced at several points in the book. For example, weak forms are practiced in the context of English rhythm (Unit 28) and connected speech (Unit 32), as well as in the section of the book (Part 7) that deals with the pronunciation of common grammar words. This recycling also, of course, helps to reinforce the various teaching points.

Order of use

Pronunciation Plus is designed for flexible use. It contains 60 units grouped into eight parts. These eight parts can be taught in any order. Here are some of the ways you could use the material:

1. Work consecutively from the Introduction through Unit 60.
2. Work through all 60 units, but not consecutively. For example, some teachers prefer to work on the more global features of pronunciation (stress, rhythm, and intonation) before individual sounds, since difficulties with these broader areas may have a more pervasive effect on intelligibility than difficulties with particular sounds. Also, stress and rhythm provide the framework within which the individual sounds fit, and inappropriate stress and rhythm may interfere with correct pronunciation of the individual sounds.

Other teachers and/or students are more comfortable working with individual sounds first. Some teachers prefer to start with vowels, since these generally present more problems than consonants do, and students with different first languages often have difficulties with the same vowels. Also, if vowels are taught first, more time is allowed in the course to practice and review these sounds. Other teachers prefer to start with consonants. Consonant sounds can be described more easily than vowels and problems may be more readily remedied, so students can start with a positive feeling of accomplishment.

3. Choose units on the basis of problems your students will be likely to have. (For shorter courses, you may need to be selective because of time limitations.) For example, problems with individual sounds, especially consonants, may vary according to students' native language backgrounds.

   For more accurate assessment of student needs, evaluate your students' pronunciation by recording each student reading a passage aloud and also doing a less controlled task; for example, describing a series of pictures. Allow students to practice the reading passage beforehand, so that they do not stumble over words and meanings.

4. Use selected parts or units of the book as problems arise with your students. For example, if you notice that students are having difficulties with word stress, you could work on some or all of the units in Part 4. If you notice that students are having problems producing a /v/ sound, you could work on Units 11 and 12.

Methodology

A traditional approach to teaching pronunciation uses a three-step procedure: discriminate + repeat + correct. So, for example, students are asked to discriminate between target sounds and then to repeat words or phrases that contain these sounds, with the teacher correcting where necessary. *Pronunciation Plus* includes these tasks, but also varies the approach and tries to move on quickly to more communicative practice. Students are asked to predict, identify, sort, match, discover rules, and exchange information. The activities are intended to help students to become more aware of their own English pronunciation and the pronunciation of native English speakers, to analyze pronunciation, and to produce various features of pronunciation in relevant contexts. Explanations are kept to a minimum in the Student's Book, with students often being asked to work out rules themselves instead.

An important feature of the book is that the activities are "task-based." They normally require students to achieve something that *also* involves them in practicing a particular feature of English pronunciation. There is extensive use of pair and group work, allowing for many opportunities for students to practice and for the teacher to circulate and give individualized feedback.

Some of the units include lists of words with target sounds, for repetition. Ask students to repeat the words aloud as a class after the tape (or after you) before calling on individual students to repeat. These lists of words are intended to help students focus on and develop awareness of the target sound (or other feature). The lists can also function as practice lists: students can be referred to the lists if they have problems with the sound in the future. Whenever possible, encourage students to add their own words to the practice lists.

Students are also asked to repeat and then practice conversations from the book, allowing for controlled practice of the target feature within a conversational framework. When students do this, discourage them from looking at the book while they read. Tell them to study their line and then look at their partners while saying it, as a way to promote fluency and a more natural intonation. Very often, students will previously have done a task (e.g., filling in blanks or matching lines to form short conversations) that will have familiarized them with the lines in the conversation and their meaning.

Monitoring

An important part of the teacher's role as recommended here involves monitoring students' pronunciation. In each lesson, the teacher should focus on the target feature of pronunciation dealt with in that unit and correct student errors involving that feature. At these points, it is best to ignore any other pronunciation errors.

Some of the tasks are controlled, with students simply repeating given language. Here it is probably best to correct on the spot, stopping students and asking them, first, to try again and then, if they make the same mistake, to repeat after you. In less controlled tasks, you may feel that it is better to note the mistake and correct the student after the task is complete. Suggestions for help with correcting specific errors are given in the individual units of this manual. If problems with pronunciation interfere with students' intelligibility, simply asking students to slow down and try again can sometimes help.

Keep in mind that it is important to offer positive as well as negative feedback so that students know when they are saying something correctly.

If appropriate for your students, encourage them to monitor one another's pronunciation. So, for example, in pair work, a student can monitor a particular feature of a partner's pronunciation, or you could appoint a third or even a fourth student to monitor the performing pair, with students exchanging roles during the practice session.

It can also be helpful to ask students to identify words, phrases, or sentences that they found difficult in a lesson. Students might write these on the board or locate them in the book. In this case, the teacher might simply say the selected item, which the student would repeat, continuing this until the student was satisfied.

Answers

Answers to the exercises are given in the teacher's notes for each unit in this manual. Scripts for any listening material on the cassettes that does not appear in the Student's Book are also included in the teacher's notes.

Background and Extension notes

In the teacher's notes for the units, *Background* information about the pronunciation point is sometimes presented. Although it is not necessary to read this information before teaching any of the units, you may find that it helps, especially in answering questions your students have. And although it is not necessary to explain any of the detail to students, you may find it useful to do so with more advanced students. It is up to you to decide whether or how much of this information to present.

Other notes give an *Extension* to the tasks in the unit. Some of these give ways of extending the task that immediately precedes, and others give a more general suggestion about how additional pronunciation practice might be provided.

Homework

Occasional suggestions for homework assignments are given in the Teacher's Manual. In addition, it is recommended that students be asked to tape-record themselves regularly, periodically (perhaps once a week) turning in the tapes for your evaluation. You could ask them, for example, to record particular exercises from the book. Feedback can be given in written form or, preferably, recorded by you on tape. Focus on errors involving the target feature and items previously taught. In the feedback, you can call attention to errors, give suggested hints for correcting them, and model the correct forms. Students could then be asked to rerecord problem items.

Vocabulary

Pronunciation Plus tries to avoid using vocabulary that is unlikely to be known by students or that is not useful to them. The vocabulary that students have to use in the activities is generally within a range that will be understood by intermediate students.

Phonetic symbols

Phonetic symbols are frequently used to represent a sound. In most cases, however, example words are also given that include this sound, so no previous ability to read phonetic symbols is required either by you or the students. A reference key to the phonetic symbols used is provided in both the Student's Book and the Teacher's Manual.

Accents of English

The accents used in the recording are those of standard speakers of North American English, without any strongly regional flavor. To provide exposure to other accents, regional accents are found in a few listening tasks in which students are not asked to repeat after the recording.

Recommended books

Here are some recommended books for learning more about English pronunciation and about helping students overcome pronunciation difficulties. Other sources are also mentioned, where relevant, in the units that follow.

Avery, P., and Ehrlich, S. *Teaching American English Pronunciation* (Oxford University Press, 1992)

Bowen, J. D. *Patterns of English Pronunciation* (Newbury House, 1975)

Celce-Murcia, M., Brinton, D., and Goodwin, J. *Teaching Pronunciation* (Cambridge University Press, 1996)

Dickerson, W. B. *Stress in the Speech Stream: The Rhythm of Spoken English* (University of Illinois Press, 1989)

Gimson, A.C. *An Introduction to the Pronunciation of English* (Edward Arnold, 1989)

Kenworthy, J. *Teaching English Pronunciation* (Longman, 1987)

Morley, J. (ed.). *Current Perspectives on Pronunciation* (TESOL, 1987)

Prator, C., and Robinett, B. *Manual of American English Pronunciation* (Harcourt Brace, 1985)

In addition, a very useful source of information about the common pronunciation problems of students with particular first languages is the following:

Swan, M., and Smith, B. (eds.) *Learner English: A Teacher's Guide to Interference and Other Problems* (Cambridge University Press, 1987)

In the introduction, students are given some ways of asking how words are pronounced and checking that they can pronounce words correctly.

You can use it in one of two ways. You can refer students to it when they try to ask you about pronunciation but have difficulty doing so in an appropriate way. Alternatively, you can teach the phrases before students start work on the numbered units in the book.

Asking about the pronunciation of written words

1 Ask students to listen to the conversations and to focus on the phrases in the balloons.

2 Students work in pairs and ask each other about the pronunciation of the words in the box, using the phrases in **1**. The words illustrate features covered in later units. The words *temperature, chocolate, accidentally, vegetables,* and *psychologist* each have a silent letter, shown here with a slash through it. Words like these are practiced in Unit 60. In *commercial*, the second letter *c* is pronounced as the sound /ʃ/ (as in <u>shoe</u>), and in *temperature*, the second letter *t* is pronounced as the sound /tʃ/ (as in <u>chair</u>). These spellings and associated pronunciations are practiced in Unit 56.

An alternative way to practice the phrases in **1** is to write a number of words that students are unlikely to know on the board. Have students come to the board, point to a word, and ask you about its pronunciation.

Another possibility is to write some difficult words on pieces of paper and distribute one to each student. Have students ask one another how to pronounce the words and reply, as in the conversations in **1**.

Asking if your pronunciation is correct

4 Ask students to listen to the conversations and to focus on the phrases in the balloons.

5 Students work in pairs and ask each other about the pronunciation of the place names given.

An alternative way to practice the phrases in **4** is to write some place names from the United States or Canada on the board. Ask individual students to have a short conversation with you, similar to the ones in the Student's Book.

Asking which pronunciation is correct

7 Ask students to listen to the conversations and to focus on the phrases in the balloons. Point out that for the words *either* and *often*, there are two possible pronunciations and that it doesn't matter very much which students use. You could ask students to make similar conversations using other words for which there are alternative pronunciations, such as the following:

economics /ɛkəˈnɑmɪks/ or /iykəˈnɑmɪks/
kilometer /kɪˈlɑmətər/ or /ˈkɪləmiytər/
aunt /ænt/ or /ɑnt/
Monday /ˈməndey/ or /ˈməndi/ (and other days of the week)
fog /fɑg/ or /fɔg/

8 For practice, have students ask you similar questions about the pronunciation of words of which they are unsure. Alternatively, write words on the board that you know cause problems for the students and have them ask you about their pronunciation using the construction in **7**.

PART 1 *Vowels*

INTRODUCTION

Aims and organization

In Part 1, students practice the pronunciation of vowels.

Unit 1   The vowels /æ/ (hat), /ɪ/ (big), and /ɛ/ (red)
Unit 2   The vowels /ɑ/ (father), /ə/ (bus), and /ʊ/ (book)
Unit 3   /ɪ/ and /ɛ/; /æ/ and /ə/
Unit 4   The vowels /iy/ (see), /ey/ (train), /ɔ/ (call), /ow/ (no), and /uw/ (two)
Unit 5   /æ/ and /ɑ/; /ɪ/ and /iy/
Unit 6   /ə/, /ʊ/, and /uw/; /ɑ/ and /ɔ/
Unit 7   /ey/ and /ɛ/; /ow/ and /ɔ/
Unit 8   /ər/ (word); vowels followed by *r* (car, short, chair, near)

The units in Part 1 are of two types. Units 1, 2, 4, and 8 present and give students practice with sets of vowels, usually vowels that share a particular feature. Units 3, 5, 6, and 7 deal with particular sound contrasts that frequently cause students problems. By organizing the material in this way, students get general practice in producing some of the main categories of vowels and then have the opportunity for more detailed practice of troublesome vowel contrasts.

If students work only on particular sound contrasts, they may learn to produce a distinction between two vowels by exaggerating or distorting one or both of them. Such distortion may interfere with the distinction between these vowels and other vowels. General categories of vowels are practiced (for example, vowels produced toward the front of the mouth) so that students develop a broader sense of the distinctions that need to be made.

Notice that not all the vowel sounds of English are practiced in Part 1. The diphthongs /ay/ (as in *ice*), /aw/ (as in *out*), and /ɔy/ (as in *boy*) are not dealt with here because they are less likely to cause difficulty than the vowels practiced. The first two of these diphthongs are practiced in Part 8 ("Pronouncing written words"), because difficulties with these sounds often involve confusion caused by spelling. The sound /ɔy/ is the least frequent vowel in English. If any of these sounds is a problem for your students, you could adapt some of the activities in Part 1 to provide practice with the sound. Some suggestions about which activities you could adapt are given in the notes for the units.

Only the stressed vowel /ə/ is practiced in this section. Unstressed /ə/ is dealt with at various other points in later parts of the book, especially in Part 4, Unit 26, and in Part 8, Unit 57.

General notes

Information on the similarities and differences between the vowels practiced is given in the notes for each unit, with descriptions of how the sounds are made. It is up to you to decide how much of this information to communicate to students. Keep in mind, though, that the precise mouth position is much more difficult to pinpoint for individual vowels than for consonants, since the lips and usually the tongue do not touch any particular point in the production of vowels. The position for a vowel is probably best demonstrated in relation to the position for other vowels, rather than in isolation.

There are often dialect differences in the way particular vowels are pronounced, and occasional sections titled *Dialect Note* are included to cover some of these.

UNIT 1 The vowels /æ/ (hat), /ɪ/ (big), and /ɛ/ (red)

BACKGROUND

The vowels in this unit are sometimes described as *lax* vowels, meaning that they are generally produced with less muscle tension in the tongue and jaws than *tense* vowels such as /iy/ and /ey/. Traditionally, these lax vowels are classified as *short* vowels. Short vowels are generally shorter in duration than *long* vowels (like /iy/ and /ey/) when they are followed by the same consonant sound (compare, for example, *sit* vs. *seat*). Also, short vowels do not occur in stressed position at the end of a word. The short/long distinction is a simplification, however, and long vowels are not always longer than short vowels. Length is affected by the consonant sound that comes after the vowel. There is more information on this in the notes for Unit 4. Note, too, that the classifications *short* and *long* can be misleading because short vowels differ from long vowels in quality (the character of the sound), not just in length.

Because of the way the vowels are produced, the three vowels in this unit are classified as *front* vowels, because they are all made with the tongue pushed toward the front part of the mouth. Of the three vowels here, the tongue is raised to the highest position for /ɪ/ (though it is not raised as high as for /iy/; see Unit 5). The mouth is a little more open, and the tongue a little lower, for /ɛ/. For /ɛ/, the sides of the tongue just barely touch the upper teeth (the bicuspids), while for /ɪ/ the tongue lightly presses against the upper back teeth. The tongue is lowest, and the mouth most open, for /æ/. To explain these positions to students, you may want to use more concrete descriptions – for example, noting that you can fit a fingernail between the upper and lower teeth when saying /ɪ/, a fingertip for /ɛ/, and a finger or pencil for /æ/.

1 If students pronounce /æ/ more like /ɛ/, telling them to open their mouths a little more may help. If more help is needed, return to practice of /æ/ later in the lesson or at another time, after students have practiced /ɛ/. Demonstrate the difference in mouth position for the two vowels, alternately saying /ɛ/ and /æ/ (or word pairs that contrast the two sounds, such as *pet/pat* or *left/laughed*) several times to show how the jaw drops for /æ/. Students should then say the sounds or words, placing a hand under their jaws to check that they are making the contrast. Suggest that students practice in front of a mirror, because the difference in mouth position is visible.

The exact pronunciation of /æ/ varies depending on where in North America a speaker is from. Some speakers make this vowel with the tongue a little higher in the mouth than the position described above and may add a short /ə/ after it, so that it sounds something like /ɛə/. Other speakers may use this pronunciation only when certain consonants follow (for example, in b_ad and m_an).

2 Answers

A: Where were you st_anding?
B: _At the g_as station.
A: Where was the m_an?
B: He r_an out of the b_ank.
A: Did he h_ave anything in his h_and?
B: A bl_ack b_ag.
A: Th_ank you, m_a'am.

Students should read the conversation to themselves and mark the vowels they expect to hear pronounced /æ/ before listening to the conversation in **3**.

Note that while *at* is said on the recording with the sound /æ/, it is often pronounced /ət/ before another word in ordinary conversation. If *at* is said on its own or at the end of a sentence, it is pronounced /æt/. (The pronunciation of words in connected speech is dealt with in more detail in Parts 5 and 7.)

6 Answers

A: Th_is one?
B: _It's too b_ig.
A: Let's g_ive her th_is one, then.
B: St_ill too b_ig.
A: W_ill this f_it?
B: Yes, I th_ink so. She's pr_etty th_in.

8 The most common problem with /ɪ/ is confusion with the vowel /iy/. This contrast is practiced in Unit 5.

10 Answers

A: And can you g_et some r_ed p_eppers?
B: How m_any?
A: T_en or tw_elve.
B: _Anything _else?
A: Some br_ead. Do you need _any money?
B: No, I'll pay by ch_eck.

12 If students have difficulty with the sound /ɛ/, have them try gliding very slowly from /ɪ/ to /æ/ and then back from /æ/ to /ɪ/. (Demonstrate this.) If they glide slowly enough, they should produce a sound something like /ɛ/ along the way. After gliding back and forth a few times, students should try stopping at the /ɛ/ sound and holding it.

EXTENSION

1. Have students make a shopping list that contains words with the three target sounds in this unit – /æ/, /ɪ/, and /ɛ/. Write the symbols for the three vowels on the board and food names underneath. For example, write *red peppers* or *bread* under /ɛ/, *fish* under /ɪ/, and *apples* under /æ/. Ask students to think of other foods for the shopping list that have these vowels. As they suggest foods, ask which column you should add them to. Students can then work in pairs and have conversations similar to the one in **10**, using foods from the list on the board.

2. Ask students how many ways each vowel is spelled in the conversation that practices it.
   Note: In **2**, /æ/ is spelled only with the letter *a*. In **6**, /ɪ/ is usually spelled *i*, but it is also spelled *e* in *pretty*. In **10**, /ɛ/ is usually spelled *e*, but it is also spelled *a* (in *many*, *anything*, and *any*) and *ea* (in *bread*).

3. Ask students to find words where the letters *a*, *i*, and *e* do *not* represent the sounds /æ/, /ɪ/, and /ɛ/ in the conversation that practices each sound. For example, tell students to look at the conversation in **2** and ask, "Do all the words with the letter *a* have the sound /æ/?"
   Note: In **2**, the letter *a* is pronounced /ey/ in *station*, /ə/ in *was* and *a*, and /ɛ/ in *anything*. In **6**, the letter *i* is pronounced /ay/ in the word *I*. In **10**, the letter *e* is silent at the end of the words *some*, *twelve*, and *else*. It is pronounced /iy/ in the combinations *ee* in *need* and *ey* in *money*, and it is pronounced /ə/ in *peppers*. Students only need to locate the examples where *a*, *i*, and *e* represent different sounds; they do not need to identify the various pronunciations.

13 Answers

1. a camera	6. a fishing rod	11. some cash	16. something to drink
2. a sweater	7. stamps	12. a tent	17. your address book
3. matches	8. a hat	13. a map	18. a blanket
4. a flashlight	9. a television	14. a tennis racket	19. an interesting magazine
5. a credit card	10. some string	15. a backpack	20. scissors

The items all include at least one of the target vowels /æ/, /ɪ/, and /ɛ/. These are underlined above. Notice that the vowels underlined include instances of *unstressed* /ɪ/, such as in the last syllable of *credit*. Often, unstressed vowels can be pronounced as either /ɪ/ or /ə/.

EXTENSION

As a follow-up activity for **15**, ask students to collect the names of things that would be useful to have when (1) cooking a meal, (2) building a house, and (3) climbing a mountain. Each word must contain the sound /æ/, /ɪ/, or /ɛ/. Ask them to report back, and monitor the pronunciation of these vowels. Make a note of the words and use them in a later lesson in an activity similar to the one in **15**.

UNIT 2 The vowels /ɑ/ (father), /ə/ (bus), and /ʊ/ (book)

BACKGROUND

The vowels /ə/ and /ʊ/ are traditionally considered to be *short* vowels (for information on short vowels, see *Background* at the start of Unit 1). The vowel /ɑ/ can be either short (as in *h*<u>o</u>*t*) or long (as in *f*<u>a</u>*ther*). While the three vowels in Unit 1 are all produced with the tongue toward the front of the mouth, the vowels in this unit are made with the tongue either in the central or the back part of the mouth.

The vowel /ɑ/ is made with the mouth open wide and the tongue very low in the mouth. Some speakers say this with the tongue in the central (not front or back) part of the mouth, others with the tongue pulled toward the back a little. For /ə/, the mouth is much less open, and the tongue rests in a neutral position in the central part of the mouth. The tongue is not pulled back or pushed forward, and the lips are parted without being either spread back or pushed forward and rounded. For /ʊ/, the tongue is pulled back a little from where it is for /ə/, and the lips are pushed forward a little, though not tightly rounded as for /uw/ (for more on the contrast between /uw/ and /ʊ/, see Unit 6).

DIALECT NOTE

British speakers have a different vowel sound (represented by the symbol /ɒ/) in many words where North Americans have /ɑ/ (for example, in *h*<u>o</u>*t*, *st*<u>o</u>*p*, *d*<u>o</u>*ll*, and *w*<u>a</u>*tch*). A small number of American speakers (especially in eastern New England) also use this vowel.

For information on dialect variation involving the sounds /ɑ/ and /ɔ/, see Unit 6.

1 If students confuse /ɑ/ and /ə/, show them that the mouth is open only a little for /ə/ but is open wide for /ɑ/. If they pronounce /ə/ more like /ɑ/, tell them to close their mouths a little. Students should try alternating between the two vowels; practice in front of a mirror can help them avoid opening the mouth too wide for /ə/. Telling students that /ə/ is a very relaxed sound may be helpful. It is the sound English speakers make when they are trying to think of what to say.

2 Answers

Note that some Americans and Canadians pronounce words such as *watch* and *wash* with the vowel /ɔ/. For these speakers, *watch* and *stopped* will have different vowels: /ɔ/ in *watch* and /ɑ/ in *stopped*.

4   Answers

1. A: Is Molly here?
   B: No. She <u>just</u> went out to <u>lunch</u> .
2. A: Do you like it?
   B: Yes, it <u>looks</u> <u>good</u> .
3. A: Does the bus <u>stop</u> here?
   B: No, on the next <u>block</u> .
4. A: Can't you <u>shut</u> the door?
   B: No, it's <u>stuck</u> .
5. A: Is that <u>blood</u> ?
   B: Yeah, I <u>cut</u> my finger.

6. A: What time is it?
   B: Sorry, my <u>watch</u> has <u>stopped</u> .
7. A: What are you reading?
   B: It's a <u>cookbook</u> .
8. A: I can't open the door.
   B: <u>Pull</u> it. Don't <u>push</u> it! /
   <u>Push</u> it. Don't <u>pull</u> it!
9. A: What's the matter?
   B: The <u>car</u> won't <u>start</u> .

7   The adjectives contain the target vowels /ɑ/ (*c<u>o</u>mmon, h<u>a</u>rd*), /ə/ (*c<u>o</u>mfortable, f<u>u</u>nny*), and /ʊ/ (*g<u>oo</u>d*). Have students practice saying the adjectives before working in pairs. Write each adjective, underlining the relevant vowel, and ask which sound it has: the sound in *f<u>a</u>ther, b<u>u</u>s,* or *b<u>oo</u>k*.

Answers

Here are some possible answers:

1. a common problem, a common name, common knowledge, common sense
2. a good book, a good movie, a good time, a good meal, a good question, a good student
3. a comfortable chair, a comfortable bed, a comfortable position, comfortable shoes
4. a hard question, a hard test, a hard job, a hard bed, hard work, a hard life
5. a funny story, a funny TV show, a funny movie, a funny joke, a funny person

---

EXTENSION

The task in **7** could be adapted to provide practice with other vowel (or consonant) sounds that students have difficulty with. For example, if you want to practice the vowels /ay/ (as in *drive*) and /ey/ (as in *train*), use adjectives containing these sounds, such as *n<u>i</u>ce, exc<u>i</u>ting, k<u>i</u>nd,* and *d<u>a</u>ngerous, f<u>a</u>mous, str<u>a</u>nge*.

UNIT 3

/ɪ/ and /ɛ/; /æ/ and /ə/

Focus on /ɪ/ and /ɛ/

DIALECT NOTE

Many native speakers add a short /ə/ sound between some vowels and a following /l/, so that *bill* and *bell*, for example, sound like /bɪəl/ and /bɛəl/. Some native speakers also add a short /ə/ sound when /ɪ/ comes before some other consonants (for example, *rib* /rɪəb/).

In the southern United States, there is usually no distinction between /ɪ/ and /ɛ/ before a nasal consonant such as /m/ or /n/. Both vowels are pronounced as /ɪ/, so that pairs of words like *pin* and *pen* sound the same (/pɪn/).

1, 2 If students have difficulty in hearing or producing a difference between /ɪ/ and /ɛ/ in the words, offer help. Say a word with either /ɪ/ or /ɛ/ and ask students to decide which vowel it has. When they get it right, ask them to repeat the word after you. You might also try saying pairs of words, either repeating a word or saying a word from each box in **1** (for example: *bill/bill* or *bill/bell*), and asking students whether the two words were the same or different. Repeat this with various pairs of words until students are usually able to tell whether the pairs are the same or different.

Tell students who produce /ɛ/ rather than /ɪ/ to close their mouths just a little; tell students who produce /ɪ/ in place of /ɛ/ to open their mouths just a little.

EXTENSION

You could adapt the task in **1** and **2** to provide practice in producing and discriminating between any pairs of sounds, either pairs of vowels or pairs of consonants.

---

3 Answers

1. B They   fell   in the hole.
2. A Can I have the   bill , please?
3. B I   left   the books at the library.
4. B It was too expensive to buy   ten .
5. A Put the file on this   disk .
6. A Is this tea   bitter ?
7. A I found a   pin   on the floor.
8. B You don't   spell   *orange juice* like that.

Focus on /æ/ and /ə/

4 Listening script

1. A black jacket.
2. Someplace sunny.
3. A hungry cat.
4. Stand up!
5. A young man.
6. Come back!
7. A traffic jam.
8. A plastic bag.
9. A lucky number.
10. A camera company.
11. Nothing much.
12. A jazz club.
13. Last month.
14. A funny hat.

Answers

Note that the target vowels are underlined.

/æ/ + /ə/	/ə/ + /æ/	/ə/ + /ə/	/æ/ + /æ/
stand up	a hungry cat	someplace sunny	a black jacket
a camera company	a young man	a lucky number	a traffic jam
a jazz club	come back	nothing much	a plastic bag
last month	a funny hat		

5 On the recording for **5**, the answers are given in the order shown in the table above: that is, first the phrases in column 1, then the phrases in column 2, and so on. This allows students to check their answers as they repeat. Monitor the pronunciation of the underlined vowels when students repeat.

If students have difficulty hearing or producing a distinction between /æ/ and /ə/, demonstrate the mouth position for each sound, first while saying the sounds aloud and then silently. Students should see that the mouth opens much more for /æ/ than for /ə/. The tongue is also clearly visible for /æ/, but not for /ə/. Telling students that /ə/ is a very relaxed sound may help.

Practice with pairs of words (such as *cat/cut, bag/bug, cap/cup*), as in **1** and **2**, can also be helpful. As a variation, have a student choose one of the words in a pair (or give the student a slip of paper with the word written on it) and say it *silently* in front of the class. Other students then try to decide which word was said.

6 Answers

The following are the most likely answers:

What did you do on the weekend?
Where do you work?
What was he wearing?
Where did you go last night?
What made you late?
Who's at the door?
When did you get married?

Nothing much.
A camera company./A jazz club.
A black jacket./A funny hat.
A jazz club.
A traffic jam.
A young man./A hungry cat.
Last month.

UNIT 4   The vowels /iy/ (see), /ey/ (train), /ɔ/ (call), /ow/ (no), and /uw/ (two)

BACKGROUND

The vowels practiced in this unit are sometimes described as *tense* vowels, meaning that they are generally produced with more muscle tension in the tongue and jaws than *lax* vowels like /ɪ/ and /ɛ/. These vowels are traditionally classified as *long* vowels. Long vowels are longer than short vowels (like /ɪ/ and /ɛ/) when they are followed by the same consonant sound (for example, *sail* vs. *sell*). And unlike short vowels, long vowels can occur in any position in a word – at the end of a word as well as at the beginning or in the middle. But the situation is more complicated than the terms *long* and *short* suggest. First, it is important for students to realize that long vowels and short vowels do not differ just in length. The vowel /ɪ/, for example, is not a short version of /iy/ but a different vowel sound. Also, the length of vowels – both short and long vowels – varies depending on the sound that comes after them. If a vowel comes before a voiceless consonant (/p/, /t/, /k/, /f/, /θ/, /s/, /ʃ/, or /tʃ/), it tends to be shorter than if it is followed by a voiced consonant or no consonant. Compare, for example, *neat/need*, *bit/bid*, *place/plays*, or *goat/go*, where the vowel sound in the first word in each pair is shorter.

If appropriate for your students, devise an exercise to make them aware of this difference in length. Give them a list of words, all containing the sound /iy/ (or one of the other vowels practiced in this unit) in the stressed syllable. Make sure that in some /iy/ is followed by a voiced consonant and in some by a voiceless one. You could select words from Units 4 and 5 and perhaps add a few more of your own, or ask students to provide you with a few. Ask them to decide which /iy/ sounds are longer and which are shorter, and why. Give a hint about the following consonant if necessary. Students might sound out the words themselves; or you could read out the list or record it on tape and give students the recording as data to be investigated. There is also practice of this point in Part 2, Unit 9.

In stressed syllables before a voiced consonant and especially when no consonant follows (that is, in positions where vowels are lengthened), the vowels /iy/, /ey/, /ow/, and /uw/ may be *diphthongized*. The mouth moves in the direction of /y/ after vowels made toward the front of the mouth and in the direction of /w/ after vowels made toward the back of the mouth. This extra "glide" sound is most evident with the sounds /ey/ and /ow/. In unstressed syllables (as in *city*, *vacation*, or *hotel*) and in stressed syllables before a voiceless consonant, these vowels are shorter and tend to be pronounced as the simple vowels /i/, /e/, /o/, /u/. Information about how the individual vowels are produced is given in the following units.

DIALECT NOTE

Many North Americans do not use the vowel symbolized as /ɔ/, or use this sound only before /r/ (as in *short*). These speakers use the vowel /ɑ/ instead. So, for them, pairs of words such as *caught* and *cot* are pronounced the same (/kɑt/). For more information, see the notes for Unit 6.

In some dialects, the vowels /iy/, /ey/, /ow/, and /uw/ are more diphthongized (pronounced with a gliding sound) than in other dialects.

1 Make sure that students make the underlined vowels long enough, especially in the words in the first, second, and fourth lines. The vowels are longest in the first line (in final position) and shortest in the third line (before a voiceless consonant).

Show how the mouth position changes for the vowels that end in glides. This will be clearest for /ey/ and /ow/; use the words in the first line (or other words where these vowels are in stressed final position) to demonstrate. Students can practice saying these words in front of a mirror. They should be able to see the mouth closing a little as they say /ey/ (d_ay_) and the lips closing and becoming more tightly rounded as they say /ow/ (kn_ow_). For /iy/ and /uw/, it sometimes helps to tell students to say the vowel twice or to write words with the sounds on the board, adding extra letters to the spelling of the vowel (for example, _treeee_).

2 Answers

	/iy/	/ey/	/ɔ/	/ow/	/uw/
1.		1 (famous)	1 (law)	2 (slow, boat)	1 (choose)
2.	2 (clean, piece)	2 (complain, great)			1 (fruit)
3.		1 (waiter)	2 (water, lost)	2 (coast, most)	
4.	1 (receive)	1 (neighbor)	2 (daughter, thought)		1 (group)
5.	1 (feel)		1 (fall)	1 (home)	2 (food, improve)
6.	1 (speak)	4 (date, delay, break, change)			

EXTENSION

Draw students' attention to the fact that each of the long vowels in the table in **2** can be spelled in different ways. You may want to write the spellings on the board. Ask students to think of one more word that contains each vowel sound. For example, for /iy/, they might suggest _me, free, believe, police,_ etc. Write the suggestions on the board, and ask students to say whether the spelling is a new one for that sound or one already shown in the table.

---

4 Answers

The correct version (matching the pictures in **4**) is given in parentheses:

One morning last April (June), Susan was still sleeping when the doorbell (phone) rang. It was her friend Dave inviting her to go to the beach for a picnic. Later that morning, Susan left her house and walked (drove) to the station to catch the bus (train). She was wearing a T-shirt and shorts (a raincoat and jeans), since it was quite warm (cool). As she sat on the bus (train), she looked out the door (window). She saw some sheep (horses) in a field. It was starting to snow (rain).

Before long, the snow (rain) stopped and the sun came out. Susan arrived at the pool (beach/sea/ocean) and met Steve (Dave). They walked down to the beach and had their picnic next to a tree (boat). They had coffee and cake (pizza and soda), and Steve (Dave) painted a picture (took photographs). They had a really nice evening (day/afternoon).

Students can use the pattern shown in **5** to say what's wrong and how to correct it. When students give corrections, monitor the vowels /iy/, /ey/, /ɔ/, /ow/, and /uw/ in the corrected words (*June, phone, drove, train*, etc.).

6 Students can retell the story either in pairs or as a class activity. They should cover up the written story, using the pictures as prompts. Monitor the pronunciation of the vowels as students retell the story. If they have difficulty contrasting vowels like /ɪ/ and /iy/ in *still sleeping* or in *picnic* and *beach*, note that this contrast is practiced in the following unit.

EXTENSION

You could practice almost any problematic vowel or consonant sound in a way similar to what is done in **4** through **6**. Make up a short story that includes words containing the problematic sound. Tell the story to the class and ask them to try to remember as much of it as they can. Then retell it, but substitute other words for those containing the problematic sound. Students stop you when they hear something different from the first version and give a correction using the same pattern as in **5**.

UNIT 5 /æ/ and /ɑ/; /ɪ/ and /iy/

Focus on /æ/ and /ɑ/

BACKGROUND

The vowel /ɑ/ is the sound a doctor tells you to say in order to see your throat, because the mouth is open wider and the tongue is lower than for any other vowel. For /æ/, the mouth is also open wide, though not as wide as for /ɑ/, and the tongue is pushed forward in the mouth, usually with the tip of the tongue touching the bottom front teeth. The tip of the tongue usually touches the floor of the mouth, not the teeth, for /ɑ/. Also, the lips are spread back a little for /æ/, but not for /ɑ/.

DIALECT NOTE

The distribution of /æ/ and /ɑ/ in some varieties of British English differs from American and Canadian English. Speakers in England, especially speakers from the southeast, use the sound /ɑ/ in many words where North Americans use /æ/ (for example, in *half, after, bath, ask,* and *dance*).

1 If students confuse /æ/ and /ɑ/, offer help. Demonstrate the mouth position for each vowel, first saying the sound aloud and then silently. Show students that they can clearly see the tongue when you say /æ/ but not when you say /ɑ/.

Practice with word pairs that contrast the two vowels (like *hat/hot*) can also be useful. See Unit 3, **1** and **2**, and the variation suggested in the teacher's notes for Unit 3, **5**.

Spelling may contribute to student difficulties with /æ/ and /ɑ/. Many learners associate the letter *a* with the sound /ɑ/ and the letter *o* only with a sound like /ɔ/ or /ow/. Call attention to the way the underlined sounds are spelled in the words in the boxes in **1**. For example, ask how the letter *a* is pronounced in these words. Point out or elicit that here the letter *a* has the sound /ɑ/ only before *r*. The letter *a* may also have the sound /ɑ/ before the letters *lm* (*calm*); after *w* or *qu* (*want, quality*); and, infrequently, at the end of a word or syllable (*ma, father*). The main point to note, though, is that *a* has the sound /ɑ/ in only a few places in English; otherwise, it has the sound /æ/ or /ey/. Ask students to think of one more word that contains each of the spellings shown for the sounds here – that is, a word where *a* spells the sound /æ/, a word where *o* spells the sound /ɑ/, and a word where *a* spells the sound /ɑ/. There is more information on pronouncing the letters *a* and *o* in Part 8, Unit 58.

2 Check that students can produce the correct question forms. To do this, have them ask you the questions first and, if necessary, write the questions on the board (for example, *Do you have a cat?*). Students will need to stand up and walk around the room to do this activity.

If your class is largely Spanish-speaking, change item 3 to *doesn't speak Spanish.*

EXTENSION

You could adapt this kind of survey task to provide practice with other vowels or consonants that are a problem for your students.

Focus on /ɪ/ and /iy/

BACKGROUND

Many learners confuse /ɪ/ and /iy/, substituting one for the other or producing a vowel somewhere between the two English sounds. The sound /iy/ is made with the tongue very high and far forward in the mouth, with the sides of the tongue pressing firmly against the upper teeth (more specifically, the bicuspids). There is very little space between the tongue and the roof of the mouth. For /ɪ/, the tongue is slightly lower and farther back. The lips are generally spread, or "smiling," for /iy/, but not for /ɪ/. The muscles of the mouth (especially the tongue) are usually quite tense for /iy/, but not for /ɪ/.

When /iy/ is longest – at the end of a word (*see*) or before a voiced consonant (*read*) – it may be diphthongized, with the tongue continuing to move forward and up a little. The vowel /ɪ/ does not have this /y/-like glide. Though /iy/ is a long vowel and /ɪ/ is a short vowel, it is important for students to realize that long vowels and short vowels do not differ just in length. The vowel /ɪ/ is not a short form of /iy/, but a different vowel sound.

4 If students have difficulty distinguishing /ɪ/ and /iy/, give extra help. If students can say /iy/ but not /ɪ/, tell them to move their tongues very slowly back and down just a little. Call attention to the tightness of the muscles for /iy/ and the way the sides of the tongue are pressed against the upper teeth. Have students concentrate on making their muscles tight as they say /iy/ and then relaxing the muscles for /ɪ/. (Clenching and unclenching your fists can help demonstrate the tensing and relaxing of muscles.) Students should be able to feel the difference in muscle tension by touching their throats just under the chin. Point out the "smiling" position of the lips for /iy/ and the more neutral, less spread position for /ɪ/; students can practice this difference in front of a mirror.

Contrast of /iy/ and /ɪ/ in word pairs such as *leave/live*, *green/grin*, and *feel/fill* may also be helpful (Unit 3, **1** and **2** can be adapted for practice).

5 Answers

India	river	cheese	Chinese	green
fourteen	knee	musician	British	teacher
milk	pink	chicken	swimming	finger
Egypt	skiing	tea	stream	a million

Spellings for the sound /iy/ usually include the letter __e__ . (Examples are *Chinese*, *green*, *knee*, *teacher*, etc.) (Exception: ski).

The sound /ɪ/ is usually spelled with the letter __i__ . (Examples are *river*, *chicken*, *finger*, etc.).

6 Answers

The following are the most likely answers:

1. things to eat	cheese and chicken
2. jobs	musician and teacher
3. countries	India and Egypt
4. numbers	fourteen and a million
5. colors	green and pink
6. sports	swimming and skiing
7. parts of the body	knee and finger
8. nationalities	Chinese and British
9. things containing water	river and stream
10. things to drink	milk and tea

7 For additional practice, ask follow-up questions as students report their answers. For example, "things to eat," *Which do you like better?*; "jobs," *Which job would you rather have?*; "countries," *Where would you rather go for vacation?*, *Where would you rather live?*; "sports," *Do you swim or ski?*

EXTENSION

Ask students to think of more words with /ɪ/ and /iy/ for some of the categories in **6**. For example, if the category is "things to eat," other possible words would include *fish, spinach, shrimp, vinegar* (/ɪ/); *beef, peas, beans, peaches, ice cream, meat* (/iy/). If the category is "parts of the body," additional examples might include *wrist, lips, chin, hip* (/ɪ/); *teeth, feet, cheek* (/iy/). Show two columns on the board, one for each vowel sound, and have students say to which column each new word should be added.

UNIT 6 — /ə/, /ʊ/, and /uw/; /ɑ/ and /ɔ/

Focus on /ə/, /ʊ/, and /uw/

BACKGROUND

The vowel /uw/ is made with the body of the tongue pulled back and raised toward the soft palate. The lips are pushed forward and rounded into a tight circle. In words like *too* and *m<u>oo</u>n*, where /uw/ is lengthened, the lips become even more tightly rounded. For /ʊ/, the tongue is pulled back, but not as far as for /uw/. The lips are pushed forward a little, but not rounded. The vowel /uw/, like /iy/, is produced with muscular tension; /ʊ/ is a more relaxed vowel. The vowel /ə/, described in Unit 2, is also a relaxed sound.

The sound /uw/ is a long vowel, while /ʊ/ and /ə/ are short vowels. As with /iy/ and /ɪ/, however, students should understand that /uw/, /ʊ/, and /ə/ are distinct vowel sounds; /ʊ/ is not a short pronunciation of /uw/.

DIALECT NOTE

In a few words spelled with *oo*, including *r<u>oo</u>f, h<u>oo</u>f, r<u>oo</u>t, r<u>oo</u>m, br<u>oo</u>m,* and *h<u>oo</u>p,* some North American speakers use the vowel /uw/, while others use the vowel /ʊ/.

1 Answers

/ə/	/ʊ/	/uw/
customer	full	include
uncle	pull	supermarket
Sunday	put	June
number	push	flu

2 On the recording, the words with /ə/ are said first, then the words with /ʊ/, and then the words with /uw/.

If students have difficulty with the pronunciation of these vowels, demonstrate the difference in lip position as you say /uw/ (tightly rounded), /ʊ/ (pushed forward a little, but not rounded), and /ə/ (lips parted in a resting position, not pushed forward or rounded). You might point out that the teeth cannot be seen with /uw/, but can usually be seen a little with /ʊ/, and can be clearly seen with /ə/. It can be helpful for students to practice the three sounds, aloud and then silently, in front of a mirror, concentrating on the differences in lip position.

If students need help with /ʊ/, they can try gliding very slowly from /uw/ to /ə/ and back again. At a point just as they move away from /uw/, they should be able to produce /ʊ/. If they pronounce /ʊ/ more like /uw/, tell them to relax the lips and not make a tight circle with them.

3 Answers

6 and 2; 1 and 7; 8 and 3; 9 and 4; 10 and 5

5 You may want to warn students that not all the words with the target sounds are spelled with the letter *u* here.

Students can work in small groups, with a time limit. At the end, see which group found the most words. Another possibility would be to assign the task for homework.

Answers

Don't worry if students miss some!
1. Where sh*ou*ld I p*u*t your l*u*ggage?
2. B*u*t I bought a n*ew* t*u*be on T*ue*sday.
3. Y*ou*'ll be t*oo* hot in the s*u*n.
4. My br*o*ther. W*ou*ld y*ou* like me t*o* introd*u*ce y*ou*?
5. Thanks. It's from a really g*oo*d c*oo*kb*oo*k.
6. There isn't m*u*ch t*oo*thpaste left.
7. In the tr*u*nk. I j*u*st have *o*ne s*ui*tcase.
8. I think I'll p*u*t on my w*oo*l s*ui*t.
9. Wh*o*'s that in the bl*ue* *u*niform?
10. That *o*nion s*ou*p was w*o*nderful.

Words to be added to the table:
Column 1 (/ə/ cup): luggage, but, sun, brother, much, trunk, just, one, onion, wonderful
Column 2 (/ʊ/ good): should, you'll, would, good, cookbook, wool
Column 3 (/uw/ two): new, tube, Tuesday, too, to, introduce, you, toothpaste, suitcase, suit, who's, blue, uniform, soup

Note that in connected speech, *should, to,* and *you* often have the unstressed vowel /ə/ instead of /ʊ/ or /uw/. The unstressed vowel /ə/ would also occur in several other words in these sentences, including *a, the, from,* and *was.*

EXTENSION

Tell students that there are four spellings that can be pronounced /ə/ in some words, /ʊ/ in others, and /uw/ in others. Draw this table on the board and ask them to write one word in each space. The word should include the spelling given on the left and the sound given along the top.

Spelling	Sound		
	/ə/	/ʊ/	/uw/
oo			
o			
ou			
u			

For example, the top row could have *blood, look, room*; the second row *brother, wolf, move*; the third row *trouble, should, soup*; and the fourth row *number, put, rule.*

Encourage students to find words that are *not* used in Unit 6. Collect the words and use them later in a task similar to that in **1**.

Focus on /ɑ/ and /ɔ/

BACKGROUND

The vowel /ɑ/ is made with the mouth open wide and the tongue very low in the mouth, either in the central part of the mouth or pulled toward the back a little. The vowel /ɔ/ is made with the tongue pulled toward the back of the mouth. The lips are pushed forward a little and rounded slightly, so that the teeth are less visible than they are for /ɑ/.

DIALECT NOTE

There is a great deal of dialect variation involving the vowels /ɑ/ and /ɔ/. Many Americans and Canadians do not use the vowel /ɔ/, or use it only before /r/ (as in *short*). These speakers use /ɑ/ in words like *caught, lost,* and *coffee,* whereas speakers who distinguish between /ɔ/ and /ɑ/ would use the vowel /ɔ/. For speakers who do not distinguish between /ɔ/ and /ɑ/, pairs of words like *caught/cot* or *caller/collar* are pronounced the same (/kɑt/, /kɑlər/).

The situation is complicated by the fact that speakers who maintain the distinction between /ɑ/ and /ɔ/ do not all use the same vowels in the same words: for example, some of these speakers have /ɑ/ in *wash,* while others have /ɔ/; some have /ɑ/ in *on,* while others have /ɔ/; some have /ɑ/ in *forest,* while others have /ɔ/; and some have /ɑ/ in *log,* while others have /ɔ/. These variations are not dealt with in this book.

6 Students are asked just to listen to the words without repeating them. Because of the widespread dialect variation that exists, it is useful for students to be aware of the two vowels, but it is perhaps not essential for them to produce a distinction between them when so many native speakers do not.

7 Answers

1. New York	4. New York	7. California
2. California	5. New York	8. New York
3. California	6. California	9. California

8 Monitor pronunciation, making sure that students do not substitute a *different* vowel (like /ow/) for /ɔ/ or /ɑ/. It is probably best for students to follow the pronunciation model of their teacher for /ɑ/ and /ɔ/.

UNIT 7   /ey/ and /ɛ/; /ow/ and /ɔ/

Focus on /ey/ and /ɛ/

BACKGROUND

The vowels /ey/ and /ɛ/ are both made in the front part of the mouth, with the tongue in a middle (not high and not low) position. When the vowel /ey/ is lengthened, it is diphthongized; in the production of /ey/, the mouth closes a little and the tongue moves up in the direction of /y/. This happens especially when /ey/ is stressed and no consonant or a voiced consonant follows, as in the words *say* or *same*. (For more on diphthongized vowels, see the notes for Unit 4.)

The tongue is a little lower and the mouth a little more open for /ɛ/ than for /ey/, and the lip and tongue muscles are more relaxed. The sound /ɛ/ is not diphthongized; it does not end with an upward movement of the tongue.

1 Answers

potato	dentist	Mexico	November	seven
eight	painter	radio	train	Asia	May
sweater	Spain	yellow	table	gray	head
helicopter	South America	bed	embassy
bread	television	dress	brain	station

2 If students do not make enough of a distinction between /ey/ and /ɛ/, show how the mouth position changes during /ey/ but not during /ɛ/: say the vowels first aloud and then silently. Students should be able to feel their jaws close and their tongues move up as they pronounce /ey/, especially in words like *May* and *gray* where /ey/ is stressed and in final position. Point out that this movement does not occur with /ɛ/. If they practice in front of a mirror, they should see the mouth closing as they say /ey/ in a word like *May*. This change can also be felt by placing a hand under the chin while saying /ey/.

3 Answers

The following are possible answers:

potato and bread: things to eat
dentist and painter: jobs/occupations
Mexico and Spain: countries
November and May: months
seven and eight: numbers
radio and television: media/use electricity
train and helicopter: means of
    transportation

Asia and South America: continents
sweater and dress: items of clothing
yellow and gray: colors
table and bed: pieces of furniture
head and brain: parts of the body
embassy and station:
    buildings/places

More advanced students could be asked to explain what the pairs of words have in common.

EXTENSION

Students could be asked to work with a partner and choose, for example, five of the pairs of words from **3**. For each, they write a question that compares the two things (for example, *Would you rather live in Spain or in Mexico?, Which country is bigger – Spain or Mexico?, Which has more calories – a slice of bread or a baked potato?, Which would you rather do – watch television or listen to the radio?*). Then they each work with a different student and ask and answer their questions. Alternatively, you could ask follow-up questions like these when students report their answers in **4**.

Focus on /ow/ *and* /ɔ/

BACKGROUND

Both /ow/ and /ɔ/ are made with the tongue pulled toward the back of the mouth. For /ɔ/, the lips are pushed forward and rounded just a little. For /ow/, the lips start in a slightly rounded position and become more rounded, until they form a tight "o" shape – much more rounded than for /ɔ/. The glide toward a /w/ sound and the change in mouth position are especially noticeable in words like *no* and *road* where /ow/ is lengthened. For more information, see Unit 4.

DIALECT NOTE

Many North Americans do not use the vowel /ɔ/ except before /r/. For these speakers, most of the words with /ɔ/ in this section would be pronounced with the vowel /ɑ/. (There is more information on this in Unit 6.)

    The vowel in words like *phone* or *coat* is usually more diphthongized in British than in American English and sounds more like /əʊ/.

5 If students have difficulty with /ow/ or with the contrast between /ow/ and /ɔ/, show how the lips close as you say /ow/ in a word like *snow*. Point out the tight "o" shape of the lips at the end. Demonstrate the difference between /ow/ and /ɔ/, showing how the lips are less rounded and do not change position for /ɔ/. If you use /ɑ/ in place of /ɔ/, the difference in mouth position will be even greater, since the lips are not rounded at all for /ɑ/. As with /ey/, students should be able to see the change if they say /ow/ while looking in a mirror, or feel the change if they place a hand under the chin.

6, 7 Students can either work in pairs first before reporting their answers, or they can work and report their answers individually. Try to elicit, by questioning, some of the target sounds in the marked words below if students do not include them in their descriptions. For example: *Where's the wardrobe?* (in the corner) or *What's in the corner?* (a wardrobe).

Answers

Words with the sounds /ow/ and/or /ɔ/ that could be used to describe the pictures include the following (not all of these appear in the boxes in **5**):

Top picture
a w<u>a</u>rdr<u>o</u>be in the c<u>o</u>rner with the d<u>oo</u>r <u>o</u>pen; a c<u>oa</u>t hanging on the d<u>oo</u>r of the w<u>a</u>rdr<u>o</u>be; cl<u>o</u>thes inside the w<u>a</u>rdr<u>o</u>be; a woman dr<u>a</u>wing; the woman has sh<u>o</u>rt hair; a man t<u>a</u>lking on the ph<u>o</u>ne; their d<u>au</u>ghter is sitting on the fl<u>oo</u>r, h<u>o</u>lding a b<u>a</u>ll; sn<u>ow</u> through the wind<u>ow</u> (or: it's sn<u>ow</u>ing); the wind<u>ow</u> shade is r<u>o</u>lled up; a desk with a dr<u>a</u>wer <u>o</u>pen; pill<u>ow</u>s on the bed; a picture of a b<u>oa</u>t on the w<u>a</u>ll; the d<u>oo</u>r of the room is cl<u>o</u>sed; the curtains are <u>o</u>pen

Bottom picture
men digging a h<u>o</u>le in the r<u>oa</u>d; a cr<u>o</u>sswalk (or: a pedestrian cr<u>o</u>ssing); a m<u>o</u>torcycle g<u>o</u>ing around the c<u>o</u>rner; a p<u>o</u>st <u>o</u>ffice; a l<u>au</u>ndromat; a h<u>o</u>tel; a cl<u>o</u>thing st<u>o</u>re with a "cl<u>o</u>sed" sign in the wind<u>ow</u>; a teleph<u>o</u>ne; a chimney with sm<u>o</u>ke coming out; a tree with leaves f<u>a</u>lling; it's f<u>a</u>ll; it's a qu<u>a</u>rter after f<u>ou</u>r; an <u>o</u>ld man w<u>a</u>lking al<u>o</u>ng – sh<u>o</u>rt, b<u>a</u>ld, al<u>o</u>ne; a t<u>a</u>ll woman wearing a c<u>oa</u>t, w<u>a</u>lking a d<u>o</u>g; people are dressed w<u>a</u>rmly because it's c<u>o</u>ld

UNIT 8 /ər/ (word); vowels followed by *r* (car, short, chair, near)

BACKGROUND

The vowels practiced in this unit are sometimes referred to as *r-colored* or *rhotacized* vowels. R-colored vowels are characteristic of the pronunciation of North American English.

Although /ər/ is written with two symbols in this book, it is pronounced as a single sound. This sound is sometimes represented by the symbols /ɚ/, /ɝ/, or /ɜr/. Unlike most vowels, which are made with the tip of the tongue down, /ər/ is usually made with the tip of the tongue pulled up and back. The tongue tip does not, however, touch the roof of the mouth. The body of the tongue is also pulled back and bunched up, forming a hollow at about the area of the soft palate.

The presence of a following /r/ in the same syllable changes the quality of vowels other than /ə/, too. In each case, the vowel ends with the tip of the tongue raised up and the body of the tongue pulled back, as for /ər/. In fact, it may be best to think of each vowel as ending in the sound /ər/.

DIALECT NOTE

R-colored vowels are characteristic of the pronunciation of most dialects of American and Canadian English. They do not occur in most varieties of English spoken in England, Australia, and South Africa (see the *Dialect Note* in Unit 14, **11**). For more information on dialects, see the note under **4** on the following page.

1 Demonstrate the sounds /ə/ and /ər/. Tell students that /ər/ is pronounced as a single sound, even though it is written with two symbols. Explain that the tip of the tongue is turned up for /ər/, but that it does *not* touch the roof of the mouth. Have students say /ə/ and, while saying it, turn the tip of the tongue up. They can try doing this both aloud and silently, to feel where the tongue is in the mouth. Use hand gestures, holding one hand outstretched with the palm up and then curling the fingers up to demonstrate the movement of the tongue; the other hand can be held above it with the palm down to represent the roof of the mouth. It can also help to ask students to make a "growling" noise, though they need to be careful not to pull the tongue too far back; the tongue stays toward the front of the mouth, raised toward the hard palate.

Point out that the underlined parts of the words in the box all have the same sound, even though there are several different spellings. The sound /ər/ can be spelled in many different ways, and students often incorrectly substitute different vowels based on the spelling.

2 Answers

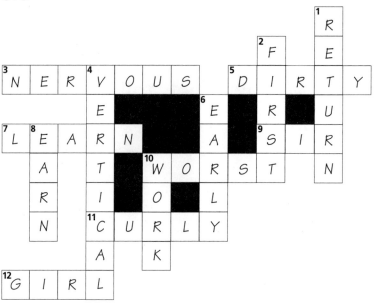

EXTENSION

Ask students to write sentences, either working in pairs or for homework, using three of the pairs of opposites in the puzzle clues and answers. For example: *I have a lot of* <u>work</u> *to do, so I find it hard to* <u>relax</u>. Then ask students to choose a sentence to read to the rest of the class.

4 Here students practice /ər/ and other vowels followed by /r/. Tell students that in each case, the vowel ends with the tip of the tongue curled up and the body of the tongue pulled back, as for /ər/. It can help to transcribe the sounds as /aər/, /ɔər/, and so on. To develop awareness of the tongue position, students can try saying different vowels both aloud and silently, turning the tongue tip up as they say them. It may be easier to start with the vowel /ɑ/ or /ɔ/, because the tongue is closer to the ending position of /ər/ with those vowels than it is with /ɛ/ or /ɪ/.

DIALECT NOTE

Note that the actual vowel sound used in some of the words here may vary. The words shown under /ɛr/ may have a sound closer to /eyr/ (for example, *hair* can be said as either /hɛr/ or /heyr/), and the words shown under /ɪr/ may instead have /iyr/ (*here* can be pronounced /hɪr/ or /hiyr/). The distinction between /ɛ/ and /ey/ and between /ɪ/ and /iy/ is lost before /r/. Similarly, the distinction between /ʊ/ and /uw/ is lost before /r/, so that *poor* may sound more like either /pʊr/ or /puwr/. Most speakers also do not distinguish between /ɔ/ and /ow/ before /r/, generally using a vowel closer to /ɔ/ in words like *bored* and *form*. Some speakers collapse the distinction between all four of these vowels (/ʊ/, /uw/, /ɔ/, and /ow/), so that *poor* and *pour* may sound alike. There is also dialect variation in the pronunciation of the vowels in, for example, *Mary, merry,* and *marry*; most North American speakers collapse the distinction between the three vowels, though some speakers pronounce all three words differently.

5 Answers

Note that the words on the recording are checked.

1. hurt ☐	heart ☑	5. bird ☐	bored ☑	9. heart ☐	hot ☑
2. shirts ☑	shorts ☐	6. burn ☑	barn ☐	10. farm ☑	form ☐
3. bird ☑	bud ☐	7. shirt ☐	shut ☑	11. ear ☑	air ☐
4. work ☐	walk ☑	8. her ☐	hair ☑	12. court ☑	caught ☐

Some of the word pairs here contrast different r-colored vowels (for example, *hurt/heart, shirts/shorts, ear/air*). Other pairs contrast r-colored vowels and vowels that are not followed by /r/ (for example, *bird/bud, work/walk, heart/hot*); these pairs often involve a difference in the quality of the vowel in addition to the presence or absence of a following /r/ (as in *work* /wərk/ vs. *walk* /wɔk/). Both types of contrast are difficult for many students, and the spelling of the vowels often adds to confusion. Note that some spellings of vowels before *r* represent vowel sounds that they never represent in other contexts.

EXTENSION

Students can practice task **5** in pairs. One partner should say one of the words in each pair, and the other partner should try to decide which one is being said. Students should take turns being listener and speaker. If students have difficulty with the pairs that contrast vowels with and without a following /r/, remind them (perhaps with a hand gesture) to curl the tip of the tongue up when /r/ follows. Students who pronounce the vowel in *work* too close to the vowel in *walk* may also be rounding their lips too much; they need to unround their lips and move the tongue forward, as well as turning the tip of the tongue up.

6 Answers

The odd one out in each line is as follows:

1. clearly /ɪr/ (The other words have /ər/.)
2. heard /ər/ (The other words have /ɑr/.)
3. wear /ɛr/ (The other words have /ɪr/.)
4. large /ɑr/ (The other words have /ɛr/.)
5. word /ər/ (The other words have /ɔr/.)

Direct students to pay attention only to the sound of the vowels, not to the spelling. You may want to do the first item with the whole class working together as an example, or you could use another group of words as an example: *first, worst, short, hurt, bird* (with *short* the odd one out).

EXTENSION

1. Give students a list of words from their course work that have vowels followed by /r/, or have students collect words that you then assemble into a list. Ask students to sort the words into groups according to how the vowels are pronounced.
2. Use a word game to practice vowels before r. Start, for example, with the word *port*, writing it on the board. Show students that you can change one letter to make a new word: *part*. Ask a volunteer to come up to the board and change – or add – one letter to make a new word (for example, *park* or *party*) and to pronounce it. Then ask another student to make a new word, continuing until students run out of ideas (for example: *port, part, park, dark, bark, barn, earn, learn*). Any letter can be changed, except for r.

8 Answers

The following are possible answers; note that they all include words with r-colored vowels.

Ernie used to have short hair, but now he has long hair.
He didn't have a beard, but now he does.
He wears an earring now, but he didn't used to.
He used to live in an apartment building, now he lives on a farm.

He used to have a small car, and now he has a large car.
He's married now, but he probably wasn't married fourteen years ago.
He used to work as a cashier/clerk in a department store, but now he's a carpenter
and makes chairs.
He used to wear a shirt and tie to work, but now he wears a T-shirt and jeans.
In the pictures at home, he's wearing shorts now and jeans/long pants in the earlier
picture.

You could also ask if anything has *not* changed. (He still wears glasses.)

Students can work together as a class, or they can discuss the pictures in small
groups (3 to 5 students) and report back to the class.

EXTENSION

Ask follow-up questions for **8** about which style of living appeals more to your
students, or have students discuss questions like the following, in groups.

Would you rather . . .

live on a farm or in an apartment?
work in a store or work as a carpenter?
have a nine-to-five job or be self-employed?
wear jeans to work or business clothes?

INTRODUCTION

Aims and organization

In Part 2, students practice the pronunciation of consonants.

Unit 9   /p/ (pay), /b/ (back), /t/ (talk), /d/ (dance), /k/ (car), and /g/ (give)
Unit 10   /t/ and /d/; /p/ and /b/
Unit 11   /s/ (same), /z/ (zoo), /f/ (four), /v/ (very), /θ/ (thanks), and /ð/ (this)
Unit 12   /θ/ and /ð/; /f/, /v/, /p/, and /b/
Unit 13   /ʃ/ (should), /tʃ/ (chair), /ʒ/ (television), and /dʒ/ (job)
Unit 14   /w/ (walk), /y/ (yes), /l/ (late), and /r/ (rain)
Unit 15   /w/ and /v/; /l/ and /r/
Unit 16   /m/ (make), /n/ (near), and /ŋ/ (long)

The units in Part 2 are of two types. Units 9, 11, 13, 14, and 16 present, and give students practice with, sets of consonants that share a certain feature of pronunciation. Units 10, 12, and 15 contrast sounds that many learners have difficulty either hearing a difference between, or producing a difference between. This organization gives learners both general practice in producing the main categories of consonants and more detailed practice with troublesome consonant contrasts. You may find that not all of the sound contrasts in Units 10, 12, and 15 are difficult for your students. Be selective and work only on those that pose a problem.

General notes

Each of Units 9, 11, 13, 14, and 16 begins with lists of words for repetition that include the target sounds for that unit. This initial presentation allows you to identify the target sounds for the learners, permits you to introduce the phonetic symbols, and provides short "checklists" that you can refer students back to if they have special problems in producing a particular sound.

Where possible, the consonant sounds are presented first in word-initial position followed by a vowel (to avoid any problems that consonant clusters might present). Words later in the lists and in practice materials use the sound in other positions – in medial or word-final position or, less often, in clusters (there is detailed practice of consonant clusters in Part 3). The exact production of a sound may vary depending on its position in a word or phrase. While it may be an unnecessary complication to draw attention to this, students do need practice in hearing and producing sounds as they occur in different contexts.

UNIT 9   /p/ (pay), /b/ (back), /t/ (talk), /d/ (dance), /k/ (car), and /g/ (give)

BACKGROUND

The consonants practiced in this unit are referred to as *stops* or *plosives*. For all of them, there is a buildup of air behind a closure at some point in the mouth and then a sudden release of the air. In /p/ and /b/, the air is stopped by closing the lips. For /t/ and /d/, the closure is made by the tip of the tongue touching the tooth ridge, or alveolar ridge (the rough hard ridge just behind the upper front teeth). For /k/ and /g/, the back of the tongue presses against the soft palate. The three different positions are illustrated in the Student's Book in **3**.

Voiced sounds are those produced with the vocal cords vibrating rapidly as air from the lungs passes between them. All vowels, and consonants such as /b/, /d/, and /g/, are produced in this way. *Voiceless* sounds such as /p/, /t/, and /k/ are produced with the vocal cords apart and not vibrating.

Note that the exact pronunciation of the stop consonants tends to vary depending on their position in a word. Voiceless stops (/p/, /t/, /k/) are *aspirated*, or pronounced with a little puff of air, when they begin a stressed syllable in English. They are not normally aspirated at the end of a word (as in *cup*) or in a consonant cluster after /s/ (as in *spot*). Aspiration involves a delay in voicing, a period of voicelessness after the stop is released and before the vocal cords start to vibrate for the following vowel. The air flows out during this period of voicelessness, sounding something like /h/ (for example, *pay* [pʰey]). At the end of a word, stops are often not released, especially if the word is last in an utterance. The speech organs form the closure for the stop, but the air is not allowed to escape.

For more on the pronunciation of /t/ and /d/ in the middle of a word, see Unit 10.

1 With more advanced students, you may want to point out the aspiration of voiceless /p/, /t/, and /k/ at the beginning of the words in the first two lines. You can demonstrate the puff of air that occurs with aspiration by holding a tissue or other light piece of paper in front of your mouth as you say a word like *pie* or *pot* (aspiration is most visible with /p/), and then comparing unaspirated /p/ in *spy* or *spot*. Explain that aspiration occurs with /p/, /t/, and /k/, the voiceless consonants in this unit. Students who do not aspirate initial voiceless stops can practice by adding /p/, /t/, or /k/ to the beginning of a word starting with /h/; for example, saying /p/ + *high* /haɪ/ to produce *pie* [pʰaɪ] or /t/ + *high* to produce *tie* [tʰaɪ]. If students hold a light piece of paper or a hand in front of their mouths, they should be able to see (or with the hand, feel) the air being let out. You can call attention to aspiration by adding a small *h* to the spelling of words: pʰay, pʰipe, tʰalk.

Note that the letter *g* does not have the sound /g/ at the end of *going*, where it is part of the spelling for the sound /ŋ/.

2 The stop consonants at the end of the words here would not usually be released, or exploded, when these words are said by themselves. Show students how the sounds are cut off, with the lips or tongue forming the sound but not letting the air out.

3 Answers

a. /k/ and /g/   b. /t/ and /d/   c. /p/ and /b/

Have students say the sounds in order to feel the position of the tongue and lips for each one as they look at the illustrations.

Ask students why it is that each picture shows two sounds. Try to elicit that one sound is *voiced* and the other *voiceless*, or unvoiced, in each pair. To demonstrate the difference between voiced and voiceless sounds, tell students to place their hands gently on their throats. First, get them to produce a long /h/ sound and then a long /ɑ/ sound (as in *f<u>a</u>ther*); ask them to note the difference. They should feel a vibration in the throat only with /ɑ/. Then ask them to repeat with the stop consonants practiced in this unit. They should feel little or no vibration in /k/, /t/, and /p/, and a noticeable vibration in /g/, /d/, and /b/.

4 Answers

Todd wants: a tennis racket, a tent, a trumpet, a television
Debbie wants: a dictionary, a desk, a dog, a dress
Kate wants: a cat, a calculator, a clock, a camera, a calendar, a cake
Gabe wants: some gloves, some golf clubs
Pat wants: a painting (or a picture), a pen, a purse
Barbara wants: some boots, some books, a bathing suit, a bicycle, a bracelet

Kate wants the most presents. (If students also list "a bookcase" for Barbara, Kate and Barbara would then want the same number of presents – six.)
Gabe wants the fewest presents.

You could go on to discuss other questions, such as *Who wants the best present(s)?, Who wants the most/least expensive present(s)?, Which present would <u>you</u> like best?*

EXTENSION

To give further practice, ask students to bring in small pictures from magazines of items that begin with the six target consonant sounds for this unit. Attach the pictures to a large piece of paper or cardboard and, at a later date, have students perform a task similar to that in **4**. You could adapt this activity to practice almost any word-initial sounds that cause students problems.

---

5 Monitor the length of the vowels as students repeat the words in the boxes. If necessary, demonstrate the difference in vowel length by a visual device; for example, use a gesture like the stretching of a rubber band to indicate the lengthening of a vowel before a final voiced consonant.

BACKGROUND

Because final stops are often not released, the difference between voiced and voiceless consonants can be hard to hear. In fact, voiced consonants like /b/, /d/, and /g/ are not fully voiced during the closure in words like ro_be_, wi_de_, and bag. The most important difference between voiced and voiceless consonants in final position is the length of the preceding vowel.

EXTENSION

Students may also have difficulty discriminating between words that have no final consonant and words that end in a stop. If this is a problem for your students, you could add word pairs similar to those in **5** to practice this distinction; for example, *play/plate, play/played, see/seat, see/seed, buy/bite, key/keep, lie/light, lie/lied, row/rope, row/robe*. Note that the difference in vowel length will be clearest in the pairs in which one word ends in a voiceless stop and the other in a vowel. Another possibility is to give groups of three words (such as *play, plate, played; sea, seat, seed; lie, light, lied; row, rope, robe*) and read them in varying order; students number the words in the order they were read.

---

6 Listening script

1. seat	3. bag	5. hit	7. hid
2. wide	4. robe	6. write	8. back

Answers

1. A	3. B	5. A	7. B
2. B	4. B	6. A	8. A

7 Make sure that students make a distinction in the length of the vowels. Discourage them from exploding the stops at the end of the words to get the difference across, and especially from adding an extra vowel at the end of the words, which may happen if they pronounce the stops too strongly.

8 Answers

1. B We bought a ___wide___ table.
2. A She's learning to ___write___ .
3. B Where can I get a ___cab___ around here?
4. B The ___robe___ is behind the door.
5. A I put it in the ___back___ .
6. B Who made the ___bed___ ?
7. A We need one more ___seat___ .
8. A The boy ___hit___ the ball.

9 Each of the adjectives in box A and the nouns in box B contains one or more of the sounds practiced in this unit. Note that the /t/ in *beautiful* and *party* is voiced in North American English. See Unit 10 for information on voiced /t/.

10 Answers

The following are sample answers:

1. something that is frightening: a deep cave, a dangerous tiger
2. something that is expensive: a good camera, a good television
3. someone who does a good job: a good dentist/doctor/teacher/cook, a patient dentist/doctor/teacher/cook
4. someone who does not do a good job: a bad (or terrible) dentist/doctor/teacher/cook
5. something you like: a colorful garden, a good dinner, a big party, a quiet dinner
6. something you don't like: a terrible pain, a bad dinner, a boring teacher

---

EXTENSION

You could extend the task in **9** and **10** for more advanced students. First, ask for more example words to go in either box A or B and write them on the board. Then ask pairs of students to write one more appropriate *Find someone/something . . .* instruction. List these on the board and ask students to use the words originally shown in the boxes, together with the additional words, to suggest answers.

UNIT 10 /t/ and /d/; /p/ and /b/

Focus on /t/ and /d/

1 Listening script

1. introduce	4. date	7. immediately
2. midnight	5. advertise	8. industry
3. pedestrian	6. stayed	9. pretend

Answers

1. t	4. d	7. d
2. d	5. d	8. d
3. d	6. t	9. t

2 This introduces the voiced *flap* or *tap* pronunciation of /t/ and /d/, which is characteristic of American and Canadian English and which is sometimes shown by the symbol [t̬] or the symbol [ɾ]. Explain that this is a very quick, short sound, and that it is voiced. Point out that /t/ is usually a voiceless sound (as in <u>too</u> or <u>tree</u>). (If necessary, see the notes in Unit 9 suggesting how to explain the difference between voiced and voiceless sounds.) Tell students to say a word like *city* or *better* with the sound /d/. Have them practice saying the word quickly, making the /d/ as short as they can. The tongue should just lightly tap the roof of the mouth.

Note that the term *unstressed* will probably be new to students. S[...]
unstressed syllables are dealt with in Part 4. For now, you could [...]
the vowel sound after the flap is very short.

BACKGROUND

The stop consonant /t/, normally a voiceless consonant, is voic[...]
North American English and sounds the same as /d/. This happens when /t/ co[...]
a vowel or /r/ and before an unstressed vowel or a syllabic /l/ in a word; examples
include *city, better, thirty,* and *bottle*. In words like *city, better* and *thirty*, the /t/ is
pronounced as a voiced flap or tap, in which the tip of the tongue lightly and rapidly
taps the tooth ridge (rather than pressing against it, as in a stop). The consonant /d/
is pronounced the same way in this environment, so that pairs like *latter/ladder,*
putting/pudding, or *atom/Adam* usually sound the same (or, if speakers make a difference it is in the length of the preceding vowel, not in the consonant). This flap sound
also occurs *between* words when /t/ or /d/ is at the end of the first word. Between words,
it can occur before a stressed vowel (as in *get up*), as well as before an unstressed vowel
(as in *out of*). The pronunciation of /t/ and /d/ as a flap before syllabic /l/ is dealt with in
Unit 21.

Though students do not need to use the voiced flap in their own speech, they need
to be aware of it in order to understand native speakers.

3 Check that students pronounce the flap in the four underlined words quickly
enough but not so quickly that it sounds as if it was omitted.

4 Answers

hot<u>t</u>est	coldest	smar<u>t</u>est	oldest	dullest	har<u>d</u>est
tallest	most exci<u>t</u>ing	most beau<u>t</u>iful		ci<u>t</u>y	

To help students decide which letters to underline, direct their attention to the rule
given in **2**. Note that there are two conditions that must be met for a *t* or *d* to be
pronounced as a voiced flap within a word. It must come: (1) before an unstressed
vowel and (2) after a vowel or /r/ (which eliminates *col<u>d</u>est* and *ol<u>d</u>est* here).

8 Though it is not necessary for students to use the flap sound, you may want to ask
students to decide whether a speaker has or has not used it in a word when
reporting back.

Focus on /p/ and /b/

9 Answers

The following are the most likely answers:

a pile of bricks
a book of stamps
a basket of pears
a piece of pie
a box of pencils
a bar of soap

a bag of potato chips
a pair of pajamas
a bottle of perfume
a bunch of grapes
a plate of pasta
a bowl of soup

11 This could be given as an assignment for homework.

/s/ (same), /z/ (zoo), /f/ (four), /v/ (very), /θ/ (thanks), and /ð/ (this)

BACKGROUND

The consonants practiced in this unit are referred to as *fricatives*. In all of them, air is forced through a small gap at some point in the mouth to produce a hissing sound.

To make /s/, the front of the tongue is near the tooth ridge (the ridge behind the upper front teeth) and the sides of the tongue press against the upper teeth, forming a very narrow groove. Air is rapidly forced through this groove, producing a strong hissing sound. The consonant /z/ is formed the same way, but /z/ is a voiced sound, so it is pronounced with the vocal cords vibrating and does not have the high-pitched hissing noise of /s/.

For /θ/, the tip of the tongue lightly touches either the cutting edge or the back of the upper front teeth. Air is forced out between the tongue and the teeth. It is not forced out as rapidly as for /s/, though, and the sound produced is quieter. The tongue is also much flatter for /θ/, leaving a wider channel for air to pass through. The sound /ð/ is the voiced counterpart of /θ/; it is made the same way, except that the vocal cords vibrate.

For /f/, the inside part of the lower lip is placed against the cutting edge of the upper teeth. The consonant /v/ is the voiced counterpart of /f/.

1 Make sure that students make the vowel long enough in words like *amuse*, *five*, and *breathe*, which end with voiced consonants. Remember that the vowel before a voiced consonant is longer than before a voiceless consonant (see Unit 9).

2 Answers

a. /f/ and /v/   b. /s/ and /z/   c. /θ/ and /ð/

Have students say the sounds as they look at the pictures, to try to connect the way the sound feels with the position of the lips and tongue shown in each diagram.

Ask students why each picture shows two sounds. If necessary, see the notes in Unit 9 on the difference between voiced and voiceless sounds. The consonants /z/, /v/, and /ð/ are voiced, and /s/, /f/, and /θ/ are voiceless.

3 Answers

Note that the words on the recording are checked.

A		B			A		B	
1. fat	☐	that	☑		8. closing	☐	clothing	☑
2. sing	☐	thing	☑		9. there	☐	fair	☑
3. say	☑	they	☐		10. Sue	☑	zoo	☐
4. some	☐	thumb	☑		11. few	☐	view	☑
5. first	☑	thirst	☐		12. prices	☑	prizes	☐
6. breeze	☑	breathe	☐		13. ice	☐	eyes	☑
7. pass	☐	path	☑		14. leaf	☐	leave	☑

4 In this activity, students have to focus on the visible features of sound production to be able to discriminate between the sounds.

Demonstrate what pairs of students need to do for numbers 1 through 9. Face the class and *silently* say either *fat* or *that*. Ask students if you said word A or B in the Student's Book. Repeat until they clearly understand the task, and then ask students to work in pairs. During pairwork, students should take turns being listener and speaker.

For numbers 10 through 14, the words in each pair differ only in that in one, a consonant sound is voiced and in the other, it is voiceless. Since this difference can only be heard, not seen, these words must be said aloud. Demonstrate this for number 10 by saying either *Sue* or *zoo* silently. Ask students if they can tell which word you said. If they answer (correctly) no, ask why not. If they think they can tell the difference, repeat the demonstration.

During pairwork, check that students make a difference in vowel length in the last three pairs (*prices/prizes*, *ice/eyes*, *leaf/leave*). If students have difficulty producing any of the target consonants, offer help, referring to the diagrams of the mouth in **2**.

EXTENSION

Students can practice at home, saying the words in each pair in **3** silently in front of a mirror.

---

5 Answers

first	February sixteenth, nineteen fifty-seven
seventy-seven	December fifteenth, two thousand and six
second	fourteenth
third	thirty-five
four hundred and forty-three	forty-six
fifth	three thousand
four thousand	

Note that the *s* in *thousand* is pronounced /z/.

If necessary, offer help with the Roman numerals in the last line. If students are not familiar with these, begin with more basic numbers, showing that X = 10, V = 5, and so on, and then showing how these combine (II = 2, XX = 20, XXV = 25, and so on). You might also want to point out the American style of writing dates, which shows the month first, then the day, and then the year.

7 Answers

1. New Year's Day: 1/1
2. Valentine's Day: 2/14
3. the first day of spring: 3/20
4. the first day of fall: 9/22
5. Independence Day: 7/4

6. Christmas: 12/25
7. Halloween: 10/31
8. Columbus Day: 10/12
9. St. Patrick's Day: 3/17
10. Veterans Day: 11/11

Before setting up pairs, go over the pronunciation of the names of holidays or events that might cause difficulty for your students.

EXTENSION

As homework, students can write a matching exercise like the one in **7** using holidays and dates in their native countries. These could be used for practice in class at another time.

UNIT 12 /θ/ and /ð/; /f/, /v/, /p/, and /b/

Focus on /θ/ and /ð/

1 If students substitute /s/ for /θ/ (or /z/ for /ð/), demonstrate the difference in mouth position, referring to the diagrams in Unit 11 in the Student's Book. Tell students to say /s/. To make /θ/, the tongue needs to move forward a little, until it is between the upper and lower teeth, with the tip lightly touching the upper teeth. It may help to tell students to relax the tongue and make it flat. Showing students that /θ/ is a much quieter sound may also help.

If students pronounce /θ/ or /ð/ as a stop /t/ or /d/, demonstrate that /θ/ and /ð/ can both be prolonged – /θθθ/, /ððð/ – with air continuing to flow from the mouth, while /t/ and /d/ cannot. Tell students to move the tongue forward a little from /t/ until it is between the upper and lower teeth. Instead of firmly touching the tooth ridge, as for /t/, the tip of the tongue should *very lightly* touch the cutting edge of the upper teeth. If the tongue presses too tightly, it will stop the air completely instead of letting it continue to escape.

2 Answers

1. A: Where's the bathroom?
   B: It's through there.
   A: Thanks.
   B: You're welcome.

2. A: When is Thanksgiving?
   B: It's the fourth Thursday in November.
   A: What date is that this year?
   B: The twenty-third.

3. A: What time's the train to Fort Worth?
   B: Three thirty.
   A: When does it get there?
   B: Four twenty-three.

4. A: Is that Tom and Matthew over there?
   B: Yes, they're always together.
   A: Are they brothers?
   B: I think so.

After students practice the conversations in pairs, call on pairs to perform one of the conversations for the whole class.

EXTENSION

1. Ask students to find other words in their textbooks that include the consonant pair *th*. For each, they should try to decide if it is pronounced /θ/ or /ð/.
2. Note that terms for many family members contain the sound /ð/, so that a family tree or family photographs would be a productive context for practice of this sound. Any context using dates would provide practice of the sound /θ/.

More practice of /θ/ and /ð/ can be found in Part 8, Unit 55.

Focus on /f/, /v/, /p/, and /b/

3 Answers

Note that the words on the recording are checked.

A		B		A		B	
1. boat	☑	vote	☐	6. pool	☑	fool	☐
2. past	☑	fast	☐	7. cup	☐	cuff	☑
3. blood	☐	flood	☑	8. best	☑	vest	☐
4. bet	☐	vet	☑	9. cheap	☑	chief	☐
5. bill	☐	fill	☑	10. curb	☐	curve	☑

4 See the notes in Unit 11, **4**, for an explanation of this activity.

If students confuse /b/ and /v/ or /p/ and /f/, give information about the way the sounds are made. Show them that for /b/ and /p/, the two lips are pressed firmly together, while for /v/ and /f/, the inside part of the lower lip is placed *lightly* against the edge of the upper teeth. For /v/ and /f/, the upper lip is not involved and does not touch anything or move; if necessary, students can hold a finger against the upper lip to make sure it does not move. Show that /v/ and /f/ can both be prolonged – /vvv/, /fff/ – with air continuing to escape from the mouth. The sounds /b/ and /p/ cannot be prolonged; the air is stopped by the lips.

Pairs that finish early could be asked to repeat the task, this time sitting with their backs to each other and saying one of the words in each pair aloud.

EXTENSION

Ask how many spellings each of the target sounds (/f/, /v/, p/, and /b/) has in the words in the box in **5**. Note that the only sound that has two spellings is /f/, which is spelled *f*, as in *food*, and *ph*, as in *telephone* or *photography*.

6 Answers

1. the printing press
2. the zipper
3. the microscope
4. the elevator
5. vaccination

6. photography
7. vitamins
8. frozen food
9. the microwave oven
10. the VCR

Students can check their answers with a partner.

7 Answers

1450	the printing press	1893	movies
1590	the microscope	1903	the airplane
1796	vaccination	1912	vitamins
1841	photography	1924	frozen food
1857	the elevator	1926	television
1876	the telephone	1944	the ballpoint pen
1884	the bicycle	1947	the microwave oven
1891	the automobile and the zipper	1975	the VCR and the personal computer

Students can work in pairs or small groups to complete the information. Regarding the phrases given in the box, note that the word *discover* would be used only with naturally existing things, like vitamins; otherwise, *invent* is used.

EXTENSION

Ask additional questions about the items in **7**; for example, *Who invented (or discovered) . . . ?*, *Which three inventions are the most important in your life?*

UNIT 13 /ʃ/ (should), /tʃ/ (chair), /ʒ/ (television), and /dʒ/ (job)

BACKGROUND

For the consonants practiced in this unit (/ʃ/, /tʃ/, /ʒ/, and /dʒ/), air is forced through a gap made between the front of the tongue and the hard palate, just behind the tooth ridge. A hissing sound is produced as the air is forced through this gap. The consonants /ʃ/ and /ʒ/ are referred to as *fricatives* or, more specifically, as *sibilants* (the consonants /s/ and /z/ are also sibilants). For the sounds /tʃ/ and /dʒ/, there is a complete closure of the gap and a slight buildup of pressure before the air is forced through the gap. These consonants are referred to as *affricates* (pronounced /ˈæfrɪkəts/); they combine the characteristics of stops (see Unit 9) and fricatives. The consonants /ʃ/ and /tʃ/ are voiceless, while /ʒ/ and /dʒ/ are voiced sounds.

1 If students confuse /ʃ/ and /tʃ/ or /ʒ/ and /ʤ/, show that /ʃ/ and /ʒ/ can be prolonged – /ʃʃʃ/, /ʒʒʒ/ – while /tʃ/ and /ʤ/ cannot. Point out that the tongue touches the roof of the mouth for /tʃ/ and /ʤ/, stopping the air completely at the beginning of the sounds, as for /t/ and /d/. For /ʃ/ and /ʒ/, the tongue is close to, but does not touch, the roof of the mouth, and the air is not stopped. Students who pronounce /tʃ/ more like /ʃ/ (or /ʤ/ more like /ʒ/) can simply add a /t/ (or /d/) sound at the beginning.

If students confuse /ʃ/ and /s/, demonstrate the two sounds, first aloud and then silently to direct attention to the mouth positions. Call attention to the fact that the lips are rounded for /ʃ/ (and for the other consonants practiced in this unit) but not for /s/. The sound /ʃ/ is also made with the tongue a little farther back in the mouth. Similar information can help students who pronounce /ʤ/ more like /dz/ or /tʃ/ more like /ts/; they need to pull the tongue back a little and to round the lips.

Note that the sound /ʒ/ does not usually occur at the beginning of words in English, except in a few words borrowed from French; no examples are included here. The word *garage* can be pronounced with either /ʒ/ or /ʤ/ at the end: /ɡəˈrɑʒ/ or /ɡəˈrɑʤ/.

2 Answers

The following are the most likely answers:

1. Where would you usually catch a train?	At a train station.
2. Where would you usually arrange a vacation?	At a travel agency.
3. Where would you usually buy a couch?	At a furniture store.
4. Where would you usually wash dishes?	In the kitchen.
5. Where would you usually keep cheese?	In the refrigerator.
6. Where would you usually study a foreign language?	At a college.
7. Where would you usually cash a check?	At a bank.
8. Where would you usually find seashells?	At the beach.
9. Where would you usually buy a gold chain?	At a jewelry store.
10. Where would you usually keep a car?	In the garage.

Model the task. Point out that students need to match the questions on the left with the answers on the right. Note that the word *usually* is difficult for many students to pronounce. Native speakers often simplify the careful pronunciation /ˈyuwʒuwəli/ to /ˈyuwʒəli/.

You might point out to more advanced students that the sound /ʤ/ would be likely to link the words *would you* in relaxed conversation. (There is more on this type of linking in Part 5, Unit 35.)

EXTENSION

For additional practice with /ʒ/, students can write questions asking about what their partner does in his or her free time. Each question should use the word *usually*, one of the most common words containing the sound /ʒ/. For example, *What time do you usually get up on weekends?*, *What do you usually do on Saturday night?*, *How often do you usually eat out?* Students then ask and answer their questions in pairs.

3 To prepare students for **4** and **5**, you could ask, *Which things in the box are good to eat or drink when you want to lose weight? Which things are bad?*

4 Listening script

Patient: So how much should I lose, then?
Doctor: Well, Joe, I would suggest at least 20 pounds.
Patient: That much? How could I do that?
Doctor: Well, let's look at what you usually eat, OK? What do you eat on an average day?
Patient: Well, for breakfast I usually have sausage and eggs and coffee.
Doctor: And for lunch?
Patient: Oh, for lunch usually a cheeseburger and french fries and maybe a milkshake.
Doctor: What else do you usually eat? Do you snack?
Patient: Well, I guess I have a sweet tooth. I like a lot of sugar. Oh, and I'm addicted to chocolate. I have to have chocolate every day.
Doctor: I see.
Patient: Is that so bad?
Doctor: Well, yes, actually, it is. I'm going to give you a diet sheet, and I suggest that you follow it. The most important things to put in your diet are fish and fresh fruits and vegetables. For example, have some fish and a salad for lunch.
Patient: Oh, fish. I like fish.
Doctor: Good.
Patient: Can the fish be fried?

Answers

The following foods and drinks from the box in **3** occur in the conversation, and students should put a check next to these words in the box: *sugar, french fries, fish, cheeseburger, fresh vegetables, milkshake, chocolate, sausage.*

5 After students practice in pairs, have them compare results with the rest of the class. Make a list of any foods they add that contain the target sounds /ʃ/, /tʃ/, /ʒ/, and /dʒ/, and have students practice saying them.

EXTENSION

Ask students to look through the words in the unit that include the sounds /ʃ/, /tʃ/, /ʒ/, and /dʒ/ and see how many different spellings they can find for each of these sounds.

Only spellings included in the unit are shown below:
    /ʃ/ can be spelled *sh (should); s (sugar); ch (champagne); t (station).*
    /tʃ/ can be spelled *ch (chair); tch (kitchen); t (furniture).*
    /ʒ/ can be spelled *s (decision, usually); g (garage).*
    /dʒ/ can be spelled *j (June); g (agency).*

There is more on the spelling of these sounds in Part 8, Units 54 and 56.

UNIT 14

/w/ (walk), /y/ (yes), /l/ (late), and /r/ (rain)

BACKGROUND

The sounds practiced in this unit – /w/, /y/, /l/, and /r/ – are sometimes referred to as *approximants*. These sounds are consonants, but they are produced without the complete closure of the stop consonants or the audible friction of the fricative or affricate consonants practiced in earlier units in Part 2.

The position of the mouth for /w/ is similar to the position for the vowel /uw/, but with the lips even more tightly rounded. The back of the tongue is raised, though the exact position of the tongue for /w/ may vary somewhat depending on the vowel that follows. Similarly, the position of the tongue for /y/ is close to the position for the vowel /iy/, with the tongue just a little higher for /y/. Both /w/ and /y/ are difficult to prolong or to pronounce alone. For both, the tongue normally glides immediately into the vowel that follows.

To say /l/ before a vowel, the tip of the tongue touches the tooth ridge behind the upper front teeth and one or both sides of the tongue are lowered to let air pass out. When /l/ comes at the end of a word or before a consonant, it is made a little differently, with the side(s) of the tongue lowered and the back of the tongue raised as if to say /uw/ ("dark /l/"). Many speakers make dark /l/ with the tongue tip touching the tooth ridge, but for some speakers, the tongue is bunched up and pulled back in the mouth without the tongue tip touching anything.

The exact production of /r/ varies a little from speaker to speaker. Typically, the sides of the tongue touch the back teeth and the tip of the tongue is raised, curling back a little and pointing toward the back part of the tooth ridge or the front part of the hard palate. The back of the tongue is usually bunched up, or raised, a little. The whole tongue may move backward a little as it forms /r/ either before or after a vowel. The lips are usually somewhat rounded, at least at the beginning of a word, though not as much as for /w/. The position of the tongue is essentially the same as for the vowel /ər/ (see Unit 8).

1 Note that most Americans and Canadians do not pronounce the second *t* in the word *twenty*.

2 Answers

The /w/ sounds are underlined. The letter *w* that is not pronounced /w/ is in *a<u>w</u>ful*, where it forms part of the spelling *aw* for the vowel sound /ɔ/.

A: <u>W</u>hat's the <u>w</u>eather like?
B: Awful. It's <u>w</u>et and <u>w</u>indy.
A: Should <u>w</u>e go for a <u>w</u>alk any<u>w</u>ay?
B: Let's <u>w</u>ait t<u>w</u>enty minutes.

DIALECT NOTE

Though some North Americans pronounce the *wh* in words like *what* as the voiceless sound /hw/ rather than as voiced /w/, in this book only the more common /w/ pronunciation is practiced.

4 If students have difficulty with /w/, have them start by saying the vowel /uw/, first aloud and then silently to feel the position of the lips and tongue. The lips are a little more tightly rounded for /w/, but should not be tight enough to stop the air.

5 Answers

The /y/ sounds are underlined. The letter *y* is not pronounced /y/ at the end of *yesterday* or *university*. The /y/ sound is not written with the letter *y* in *interview* /ˈɪntərvyuw/, *university* /ˌyuwnəˈvərsəti/, or *music* /ˈmyuwzɪk/.

A: I had an interview yesterday.
B: At the university?
A: Yes. In the music department.
B: Do you know if you got the job?
A: No, I don't know yet.

7 If students pronounce /y/ like /dʒ/, point out the difference in the way these conso-nants are made. For /dʒ/, the tip of the tongue goes up to the roof of the mouth and stops the air completely. For /y/, the tip of the tongue does not touch the roof of the mouth at all, and the shape of the tongue is flatter. Also, the lips are rounded for /dʒ/, but not for /y/; say a pair of words like *jet/yet* to demonstrate. In fact, the posi-tion of the tongue for /y/ is much more like the position for the vowel /iy/ than for the consonant /dʒ/. Get students to say the vowel /iy/ and to hold this sound, feeling where the tongue is. Students who tend to replace /y/ with /dʒ/ can try saying the vowel /iy/ at the beginning of a word like *yes* or *you* and moving quickly into the next vowel. The /y/ sound should be smoothly linked to the following vowel.

8 Answers

The /l/ sounds are underlined. The letter *l* is not pronounced /l/ in the word *would*; it is silent.

A: Would you like to have lunch?
B: It's a little early.
A: It's almost twelve o'clock.
B: Let's wait till twelve thirty.
A: Well, OK. But no later, or I'll be late for class.

Note that in connected speech, the *l* in *almost* is often not pronounced.

10 If students have difficulty pronouncing /l/, the following information about how to make this sound may help them. Show students that the tip of the tongue touches the ridge behind the upper front teeth and that one or both sides of the tongue are down. To help students get a clearer feeling for this position, tell them to say a long /lll/ sound and then, keeping the tongue in the same place, to breathe in. They should feel the air coming in over the side(s) of the tongue. They can alternate saying a long /sss/ and a long /lll/, breathing in after each sound to feel the differ-ence. Note that the tongue moves quickly away from the roof of the mouth to form a vowel after /l/.

Many students have difficulty with "dark /l/" (see **Background** at the beginning of this unit). Some students tend to omit /l/ before a consonant (e.g., in *cold*) or to pronounce final /l/ (e.g., in *well*) as a back vowel (a vowel made with the tongue pulled toward the back of the mouth) like /ow/ or /uw/. Sometimes /l/ in these contexts sounds more like /w/. It may be best for these students to make sure to pronounce dark /l/ with the tip of the tongue touching the roof of the mouth, even though native speakers do not always do this. In addition, point out the difference in the position of the lips – rounded for /w/ and the back vowels but not rounded for /l/.

DIALECT NOTE

> The exact pronunciation of /l/, as well as the contexts in which "dark /l/" is used, differs from dialect to dialect. For example, many North Americans use dark /l/ between two vowels (e.g., in *silly*), but some speakers do not. There is usually a greater difference between the pronunciation of /l/ at the beginning of a word and at the end of a word in British English than in American English.

11 Answers

The /r/ sounds are underlined.

A: Did you <u>r</u>emembe<u>r</u> to call <u>R</u>ay?
B: I t<u>r</u>ied th<u>r</u>ee times on F<u>r</u>iday.
A: He was p<u>r</u>obably at the lib<u>r</u>a<u>r</u>y.
B: You'<u>r</u>e p<u>r</u>obably <u>r</u>ight. I'll t<u>r</u>y again tomo<u>rr</u>ow.

DIALECT NOTE

> In this book, the model of pronunciation used is North American English. In most American and Canadian dialects, the letter *r* is pronounced in all positions. In most varieties of English spoken in England, Australia, and South Africa, however, as well as a few dialects of English spoken in North America, the letter *r* is not pronounced in these cases: (1) when it is followed by a consonant, as in the word *a<u>r</u>m*; and (2) when it is not followed by any other sound – that is, at the end of a word (e.g., in *docto<u>r</u>*) or before a silent letter *e* (e.g., in *ca<u>r</u>e*). If your students are likely to have contact with speakers of accents in which the letter *r* in these positions is *not* pronounced (accents that are sometimes referred to as *non-rhotic*), point this feature out to them.

13 Explain that to make an English /r/ sound, the tip of the tongue points to the roof of the mouth but does not actually touch it. Demonstrate a word with initial /r/ (like *<u>r</u>ight*), showing students that the lips are rounded a little for /r/. (If students produce a sound closer to /w/, they may be rounding their lips *too* tightly. Also, the tongue tip points *down* for /w/, but *up* for /r/.) It may help for students to start by saying a vowel sound like /ə/ or /ɑ/ and then slowly raise and curl back the tongue until they reach an /r/ sound. Or they can start with a vowel like /iy/ or /ɪ/, where the sides of the tongue touch the upper back teeth (as for /r/), and curl back only the tip of the tongue. To say /r/ at the beginning of a word, students should also round their lips. If students can produce /ər/ (Unit 8), tell them to say this sound quickly, moving smoothly into the vowel that follows.

Note that in many other languages, the tip of the tongue touches the roof of the mouth for /r/, producing a sound more like the flap heard in *city* (see Unit 10). You may want to contrast the two sounds in word pairs like *hea<u>r</u>ing/heating, be<u>rr</u>y/Betty*.

14 Listening script

Will: Hi, Laura.

Laura: Hi, Will.

Will: I didn't see you last week. Were you away?

Laura: Yeah, I went to Florida.

Will: Oh, really? Did you go by yourself or –

Laura: No, I went with – um, a friend – someone I work with.

Will: Where did you go?

Laura: Well, we went to a small island, on the west coast.

Will: Where did you stay?

Laura: Just a small hotel. It was, you know, nothing luxurious, but it was clean and very quiet.

Will: Sounds wonderful.

Laura: It was – it really was.

Will: What did you do? Was there much to do there?

Laura: Well, the hotel was, like, right on the water. We went swimming a lot, and I tried windsurfing.

Will: Oh, I've always wanted to try that.

Laura: It was lots of fun. You'd like it.

Will: How was the weather?

Laura: Well, it wasn't very warm. Actually, it was pretty cool. But it didn't rain, at least.

Will: Well, you look great.

Answers

Where?	Florida
With whom?	with a friend
Hotel?	small, clean, quiet
Things to do?	swimming, windsurfing
Weather?	cool

15 Have students practice the pronunciation of the words in the boxes on the right of the table before they begin pairwork. Focus on the pronunciation of the target sounds – /w/, /y/, /l/, and /r/. Point out that the sound /w/ is not always spelled with the letter *w* (for example, in *quiet*) and that /y/ occurs in *museums* and *beautiful*.

Model the example conversations. Check that students can produce appropriate questions to ask for the information. If necessary, write the questions on the board. There is often more than one way to ask for the information (for example, *Who did you go with?* or *Did you go by yourself?*). After pairwork, select some pairs to perform their conversations for the class.

EXTENSION

Additional questions for students to use in discussing their imaginary vacations in **15** could include *When did you go?* (last week, last year, in the spring, in the fall) or *How did you travel?* (by car, by train, by plane, we drove).

UNIT 15 — /w/ and /v/; /l/ and /r/

Focus on /w/ and /v/

1 Answers

1. 2 I only have twelve.
2. 1 She works hard every day.
3. 2 We had to drive up on the sidewalk to avoid him.
4. 2 I lost my wallet, traveler's checks, and visa.
5. 3 We're having visitors over the weekend.

3 For information about the pronunciation of /v/, see the notes for Units 11 and 12.

4 Answers

1. 2 What's this one over here?
2. 2 Was everything made of wood?
3. 2 It's quite warm for November.
4. 3 They're having a quiet wedding next Wednesday.
5. 4 It was very wet last week, wasn't it?

6 If students confuse /v/ and /w/, point out that the upper teeth touch the lower lip for /v/ but do not touch the lower lip for /w/. Show them that you can see the front teeth with /v/, but not with /w/. Contrast the two sounds in word pairs like *west/vest* or *we/V*. Try saying one of the words in such a pair *silently*; students should decide which word you said. Some students may tend to substitute the sound /g/ for /w/ in some words (such as *would*). The back of the tongue is raised for both sounds, but in /w/ it is not raised enough to press against the roof of the mouth and stop the air as it does in /g/.

Focus on /l/ and /r/

7 Answers

a. /r/   b. /l/

8 If students have difficulty producing a distinction between /l/ and /r/, point out these differences in the way these sounds are made, referring to the pictures in **7** where appropriate:

1. To make /l/, the tip of the tongue touches the roof of the mouth, at the ridge just behind the front teeth. To make /r/, the tip of the tongue points toward the roof of the mouth, but it does not touch it (or anything else).
2. For /l/, one or both sides of the tongue are down to let air escape. For /r/, the sides of the tongue are raised, touching the back teeth; air goes out over the middle of the tongue, not over the sides.
3. The lips are rounded a little for /r/, especially before a vowel; they are not rounded for /l/.
4. For /l/, one or both sides of the tongue do not touch anything. For /r/, the tip of the tongue does not touch anything.

Practice with word pairs such as _light/right, long/wrong, collect/correct, glass/grass_ can be helpful. There are many such pairs in English.

9 Explain the task. Students work in pairs to decide which sentence gives the meaning of each road sign. Offer help with the vocabulary if necessary, going over any new words before asking students to work in pairs.

Answers

1. No right turns are allowed.
2. The road is slippery when it rains.
3. The road will get narrower on the right.
4. You are coming to a hill.
5. Schoolchildren cross the street here.
6. You are coming to a railroad crossing.
7. Keep right.
8. At the sign, let other traffic go first.
9. Traffic will enter from the right.
10. You are coming to a traffic light.

10 When students compare answers, instead of having them read the answers as given in the Student's Book, you could ask them to cover the sentences on the right and say what each sign means using their own words.

EXTENSION

Any activity that practices asking for and giving directions will almost certainly include practice of /l/ and /r/. For example, ask each student to write the name of a well-known place in your town or city (a particular store, park, museum, and so on) on a small piece of paper. Collect the slips of paper and put them into a box. Each student then takes a piece of paper and asks for directions to the place, with other students volunteering directions.

UNIT 16 /m/ (make), /n/ (near), and /ŋ/ (long)

BACKGROUND

The three sounds practiced in this unit are referred to as *nasal* consonants because the air is pushed out of the nose. For each, there is a closure at some point in the mouth while air is allowed to go out through the nose. For /m/, the closure is made by the two lips; for /n/, the tip of the tongue touches the tooth ridge behind the upper front teeth; and for /ŋ/, the back of the tongue is raised to touch the soft palate (the same position used in making /k/ and /g/). Notice that the sound /ŋ/ does not occur at the beginning of English words, but is found between vowels and also very frequently at the end of words.

1 Make sure that students pronounce nasal consonants clearly at the end of a word or syllable. Sometimes students make final nasal consonants too weak or use a nasalized vowel instead. Some students do not make enough of a distinction between the three nasal consonants at the end of a word, or use a different nasal consonant in place of the correct one. If necessary, point out the difference in the position of the lips and tongue for the three sounds. These are the same three positions shown for the stop consonants in the pictures in Unit 9, **3**.

If students replace final /m/ with /n/ or /ŋ/, tell them to press their lips together. If they replace /n/ with /ŋ/, tell them to press the tip of the tongue against the ridge just behind the upper front teeth.

2 Answers

The target consonants are underlined below.

1. He's pai<u>n</u>ti<u>ng</u>.
2. He's doi<u>ng</u> lau<u>n</u>dry.
3. He's clea<u>n</u>i<u>ng</u> the bathroo<u>m</u>.
4. He's iro<u>n</u>i<u>ng</u>.
5. He's shoppi<u>ng</u>.
6. He's garde<u>n</u>i<u>ng</u>.
7. He's cooki<u>ng</u>.
8. He's washi<u>ng</u> dishes.
9. He's joggi<u>ng</u>.
10. He's vacuumi<u>ng</u> the livi<u>ng</u> roo<u>m</u>.
11. He's liste<u>n</u>i<u>ng</u> to <u>m</u>usic.

Note that in relaxed speech, many native speakers pronounce the ending *-ing* as /ɪn/ or /ən/ (or as a syllabic /n̩/ where this is possible, as in *eating* /ˈiytn̩/). This ending is sometimes written informally as *-in'* (e.g., *cookin'*). You may want to make more advanced students aware of this pronunciation, though it is probably best for learners to use /ŋ/ in their speech.

4 Answers

These are the answers students should give as they work in pairs.

1. He likes painting.
2. He doesn't like doing laundry.
3. He doesn't like cleaning the bathroom.
4. He likes ironing.
5. He doesn't like shopping.
6. He likes gardening.
7. He likes cooking.
8. He doesn't like washing dishes.
9. He doesn't like jogging.
10. He likes vacuuming the living room.
11. He likes listening to music.

EXTENSION

Have students work in pairs or small groups and ask each other whether they like or dislike doing the things shown in **2**. You may want to include other household chores for more variety in verbs. Ask students to name other chores around the house (for example, washing windows, drying dishes, washing floors, sweeping, taking out the garbage, mowing the lawn, shoveling snow). Students can discuss which chores they like/don't mind/don't like doing, or they can rank them in order of preference. After students report what they have found, they can decide which activities were the most and least popular, perhaps noting whether there were differences in men's and women's preferences.

5   Explain the activity. Each student chooses three classmates to talk to, and writes their names in the spaces at the top. Students then talk to these three people, asking questions about what they do on weekends. Students will probably need to get up and walk around the room to do this.

Go over any new vocabulary. Model the example questions and answers with a student. For each answer, ask students what to write in the column under that person's name. For example: Teacher: *Do you ever go mountain climbing?*
Student: *No, never;* write *N.* Set a time limit for the activity (about 10 minutes).

EXTENSION

When students report their findings in **6**, you could ask, for example, if there were activities that only one person did. You could also ask students what activities they do on weekends that were *not* included in the table.

PART 3 *Consonant clusters*

INTRODUCTION

Aims and organization

In Part 3, students practice consonant clusters at the beginning of words, at the end of words, and in the middle of words. They also practice syllabic consonants at the end of words.

Unit 17   Consonant letters and consonant sounds (distinguishes between consonant letters and consonant sounds and introduces the idea of a consonant cluster)

Unit 18   Consonant clusters at the beginnings of words

Unit 19   More on consonant clusters at the beginnings of words

Unit 20   Consonant clusters at the ends of words

Unit 21   Syllabic consonants; more on consonant clusters at the ends of words

Unit 22   Groups of consonants in the middle of words; simplifying final consonant clusters (practices sequences of consonants in the middle of words, especially ones that may not be apparent from the spelling, and points out some ways that final consonant clusters are simplified in normal speech)

General notes

A *consonant cluster* occurs when two or more consonant sounds occur within one syllable without an intervening vowel sound. Notice that a consonant cluster isn't always found where there are two written consonant letters: for example, the word *shoe* begins with two consonant letters but only one consonant sound.

A *syllabic consonant* occurs when a consonant forms a syllable in itself without any vowel sound, as at the end of the word *bottle* (with syllabic /l/) or *sudden* (with syllabic /n/).

BACKGROUND

Different languages allow different possible combinations of consonants in clusters. So, for example, /zd/ is not a possible cluster at the beginning of an English word though it is possible in Russian.

Consonant clusters may be possible in some positions in words but not in other positions. For example, /ps/ is possible at the end of an English word (e.g., *caps*), but not at the beginning. For details of possible consonant clusters at word beginnings and ends in English, see Prator and Robinett (1985, pp. 175–179), in the list of recommended books at the end of the introductory section To the Teacher. Many more sequences of consonants, of course, are possible in the middle of words and across word boundaries – where a sequence can be broken up between syllables – than at the beginnings and ends of single words – where the consonants must be said together within a single syllable.

Unit 17 Consonant letters and consonant sounds

The idea of a consonant cluster is introduced in the first paragraph of Part 3 in the Student's Book. To check that students have understood, write words on the board that include consonant clusters at the beginning or at the end. Select students to come to the board to underline the consonant clusters in each word.

1, 2 Answers

	Number of consonant letters	Number of consonant sounds		Number of consonant letters	Number of consonant sounds
1. blood	2	2 (/bl/)	7. right	3	1 (/t/)
2. against	3	3 (/nst/)	8. next	2	3 (/kst/)
3. ticket	2	1 (/k/)	9. there	2	1 (/ð/)
4. school	3	2 (/sk/)	10. walk	2	1 (/k/)
5. dollar	2	1 (/l/)	11. film	2	2 (/lm/)
6. chair	2	1 (/ʧ/)	12. street	3	3 (/str/)

Draw attention to the fact that the number of consonant *sounds* may differ from the number of consonant *letters*.

3 Answers

The following are possible answers. Note that the "Xs" should appear as shown, while the example words may vary:

	/l/	/m/	/r/
/k/	clock	X	cry
/d/	X	X	dress
/g/	glass	X	grapes
/p/	plug	X	prize
/s/	slow	small	X
/t/	X	X	triangle

Consonant clusters / Part 3

Note that /sr/ can occur in *Sri Lanka*, but this is the only word beginning with this cluster that is regularly used in English.

4 If students identify particular pronunciation problems that they have, ask them to consider why this might be. The reason is most likely that the consonant cluster doesn't occur in their own language. However, it isn't always the case that consonant clusters that don't occur in a student's native language cause difficulties when they occur in English. You might want to make a note of difficulties that students say they have in order to focus on them in future practice.

6 This is an "around-the-class" activity. Point out that one of the consonant sounds is repeated in the consonant cluster beginning the next word.

To check that students have understood, ask for suggestions on how the chain given in the book might continue (for example, *prize*, which starts with a consonant cluster that includes /p/). Start a new chain by giving a word yourself and asking for a suggestion for the next word. Continue to ask for suggestions as the chain grows, or call on students. A student who gives a wrong word or a repeated word is eliminated. Keep a note of words that cause problems, and at the end of the activity, check that students can pronounce them correctly.

UNIT 18 Consonant clusters at the beginnings of words

BACKGROUND

The articulation of the consonants in a cluster often overlaps. For example, if the first consonant is voiceless (e.g., /p/, /t/, or /k/), the voicelessness often carries over into the beginning of a following consonant that is normally voiced (e.g., /l/, /r/, or /w/), as in *practice*, *try*, *clock*, or *quite*. Or the overlap may extend in the opposite direction, with the speech organs moving into position for the second sound while articulating the first sound. Compare, for example, the position of the lips in saying the /t/ of *try* (slightly rounded in preparation for /r/) and *tie* (not rounded) or in saying the first /k/ of *quick* (rounded for /w/) and *kick* (not rounded). Notice that in /tr/ and /dr/ clusters, the first consonant often sounds more like an affricate /tʃ/ or /dʒ/ than a stop /t/ or /d/, with the affricate sound produced as the tongue moves away from the roof of the mouth for /t/ or /d/ to form /r/.

Note, too, that a voiceless stop (/p/, /t/, or /k/) is not aspirated (pronounced with a small puff of air) when it follows /s/ in a cluster; compare *stop/top*, *sport/port*. These stops *are* aspirated, however, when they begin a cluster, as in *practice*, *try*, *clock*, or *quite*. (For more on aspiration, see Unit 9.)

1 During repetition, make a note of which clusters cause problems for which students. Not all clusters will be difficult for all students.

Students who have difficulty with initial clusters may add a vowel between the consonants (e.g., "caream" for *cream*) or before the consonants (e.g., "estop" for *stop* in **4**). Or they may simply drop one of the consonants (or, if they make the second consonant too short, it may sound as if it were dropped). If one of the sounds in the cluster – for example, /l/ or /r/ – is difficult for students, they may substitute a different consonant.

It can help to tell students to form the second consonant or to say the second consonant silently first, and *then* to say the word aloud.

2 Answers

C	A	B	R	O	T	H	E	R	E
O	C	L	O	C	K	T	R	I	P
P	L	A	S	T	I	C	A	L	L
R	E	N	T	I	P	R	Q	E	A
A	A	K	E	C	L	O	U	D	Y
C	R	E	A	M	A	W	I	D	E
T	L	T	R	I	C	D	C	E	D
I	Y	O	B	R	E	A	K	A	P
C	E	Q	U	A	R	T	E	R	E
E	W	O	R	D	S	C	R	Y	N

4 Again, during repetition, make a note of which clusters cause problems for which students. See the discussion under **1**.

If students add a vowel before an initial cluster with /s/ (as in *stop*), have them start by making a very long /s/ sound (e.g., /ssstɑp/); they should concentrate on saying /s/ and making sure the tip of the tongue stays up.

Use A to G in **1** and H to M in **4** as practice lists. Refer students back to the lists if they have particular problems with word-initial consonant clusters in the future.

EXTENSION

The consonant clusters practiced in the lists in **1** and **4** are among the most common in English, but many others are possible. If you notice that your students have problems with a cluster not given in **1** or **4** (for example, /sm/ in *smile* or *smoke*), write your own list of words beginning with the problem cluster. You might hang a large version of the list on a wall in the classroom, and have students repeat the words in the list each time they make a mistake in pronouncing the cluster.

---

5 Answers

The following are the most likely answers:

How many tickets do you want?	Three, please.
What did you buy at the mall?	A <u>cl</u>ock and some new <u>sl</u>ippers.
Should we take the bus?	No, let's <u>dr</u>ive. It's <u>qu</u>icker.
Where should we meet?	At the <u>br</u>idge by the <u>st</u>ation.
Oh, no, I missed it.	Don't worry. There are <u>pl</u>enty more <u>tr</u>ains tonight.
He can't understand my English.	<u>Tr</u>y <u>sp</u>eaking more <u>sl</u>owly.
What do you like best on TV?	<u>Sp</u>orts <u>pr</u>ograms and <u>thr</u>illers.
What instruments do you play?	The <u>tr</u>umpet and the <u>dr</u>ums.

EXTENSION

Ask students to work in pairs to collect more words containing the clusters practiced in this unit (or particular clusters that cause problems) from the Student's Book or their other textbooks. They can then write two-line conversations similar to the ones in **5**, including the words, and say these conversations for the rest of the class. Or you could collect the conversations they have written and use them to practice these sounds at a later date.

UNIT 19   More on consonant clusters at the beginnings of words

1 Answers

1. Is the ___clock___ broken?
2. They'll ___grow___ much higher than that.
3. I learned to ___drive___ last summer.
4. Should we ___pay___ now or later?
5. How much money did you ___spend___?
6. How many have you ___bought___?
7. The ___plane___ was terrible.
8. Are you sure it's ___true___?
9. Did you ___say___ two weeks or three?
10. He's been a good ___support___.

Students have to discriminate between words that begin with a consonant cluster and words that begin with a single consonant sound. The last pair contrasts a consonant cluster (/sp/) and the same sequence of two consonants separated by an intervening vowel.

2 You may want to demonstrate the task first. Say, for example, *Is the lock broken?*, and ask students if you are using a word from box A or B. Then students work in pairs.

If students find a word in box A difficult to pronounce, it may help to have them practice saying the corresponding word in B first, and then the word in A (for example, *lock – clock*). If students have difficulty with pairs like *sport/support* (that is, if they tend to insert a vowel between consonants in a cluster like /sp/), you may want to give them more practice with similar pairs; for example, *claps/collapse, prayed/parade, blow/below, star/sitar*. Note that the intervening vowel in the second word in these pairs is very short.

EXTENSION

If students insert a vowel before clusters beginning with /s/ (for example, pronouncing *stay* as "estay"), have them practice sentences like those below, following the same directions as in **2**.

She lives near _____. (school/a school)

Is it _____? (square/a square)

I did _____ last semester. (study/a study)

He left the _____. (state/estate)

The baby's _____ in the living room. (sleeping/asleep)

---

3 Answers

1. a dress
2. a frying pan
3. flippers
4. a swimsuit

5. gloves
6. a clock
7. a sweater
8. a sleeping bag

9. a scarf
10. a ski suit
11. bug spray
12. skis

13. a plate
14. a flashlight
15. slippers
16. a credit card

4 During repetition, monitor the pronunciation of the consonant clusters underlined above.

5 Listening script

Brandon: Hello?

Stephanie: Hi, Brandon.

Brandon: Oh, Stephanie, hi. How's it going?

Stephanie: OK. I wanted to ask you a couple of questions. I'm going skiing next week and I wanted to ask your advice about what to take. I'm taking a ski suit and gloves, obviously.

Brandon: Yeah, you'll need good gloves. You'll definitely need those. If you have your own skis, too, that could save you a lot of money because otherwise you have to rent them and it's really expensive. Where are you going to stay?

Stephanie: Oh, I'm staying in a hotel. A pretty big one, I think.

Brandon: Well, in that case, you should probably take a swimsuit because most of the big hotels . . . they usually have an indoor pool . . .

Stephanie: Oh, that's a good idea.

Brandon: . . . it's really relaxing, you know, to go for a swim after skiing all day.

Stephanie: Do you think I'll be warm enough in a ski suit? I mean, without a jacket on top?

Brandon: Yeah, I think so. I mean, if you have a ski suit and a warm sweater and maybe a scarf. Yeah, you should be OK with that.

Stephanie: So no jacket . . .

Answers

Students should put a check next to the following items: a swimsuit, gloves, a sweater, a scarf, a ski suit, skis

6 You may want to demonstrate a conversation with a student before you ask students to work in pairs. Use some of the phrases given in the box during your demonstration and talk about as many of the items in the pictures on page 45 in the Student's Book as you can.

EXTENSION

At a later time, you could do an exercise similar to the one in **6**, focusing on particular consonant clusters that cause problems for some or all of your students. For example, if you have noticed that some of your students have difficulty pronouncing words beginning with /br/ and /bl/, make a list of things beginning with these sounds (for example, *bread, a broom, a bracelet, a blanket, a blouse*). Ask students to discuss which they would buy as a present for a son/daughter/mother, and so on, or which they would usually find in the kitchen/bedroom/, or other room.

UNIT 20 Consonant clusters at the ends of words

BACKGROUND

Many more different consonant clusters are allowed at the end of a word in English than at the beginning, and these clusters can have up to four consonants. Many of the more complicated clusters occur when a grammatical *-s* or *-ed* ending is added to a word, as in *sixths* /sɪksθs/ or *changed* /tʃeyndʒd/. Consonant clusters formed by adding *-ed* and *-s* endings are for the most part avoided in this unit; they are dealt with in more detail in Units 51 and 52.

1 Answers

Note that the words on the recording are checked.

	A		B			A		B	
1.	belt	☐	bell	☑	6.	card	☑	car	☐
2.	field	☑	feel	☐	7.	cold	☑	code	☐
3.	start	☑	star	☐	8.	needs	☐	knees	☑
4.	nights	☐	nice	☑	9.	fault	☐	fall	☑
5.	built	☑	bill	☐	10.	think	☑	thing	☐

3 Listening script

since, want, garden, friend, called, silence, isn't, understand, pronounce, listen, thousand, once, important, conversation, tennis, find, minute, different, eleven

Answers

/ns/	/nt/	/nd/
since silence pronounce once	want isn't important different	friend understand thousand find

4 When students repeat the words as they check their answers, make sure that they do not drop the /n/ in the clusters; the tongue should touch the tooth ridge for /n/.

BACKGROUND

When /nd/ comes at the end of a word said on its own, the final /d/ is usually not released. The tongue forms the closure for the stop consonant and stays there without moving away to let the air escape. In connected speech, the pronunciation of the cluster /nd/ varies depending on what follows. If the next word begins with a vowel sound, the /d/ is usually linked to the vowel (as in *find out*). If the next word begins with a consonant, the final /d/ may be dropped (as in *find me*) or may merge with the consonant sound that follows (as in *send food*).

When /nt/ comes at the end of a word said on its own, the /t/ may be unreleased, like /d/ in /nd/, or pronounced together with a glottal stop (the sound heard at the beginning of each syllable in *uh-oh*). Before a vowel (as in *want it*), the /t/ in /nt/ is dropped by many North American speakers. If the next word begins with a consonant, the final /t/ may merge with the consonant sound that follows (as in *want them*) or may be accompanied or replaced by a glottal stop (as in *want one*; for more information on glottal stops, see Unit 21).

Note that in the cluster /ns/, an extra /t/ sound is often inserted in passing from /n/ to /s/ (for example, *since* /sɪnts/).

5 Answers

How long have you been here?	<u>Since</u> Wednesday.
How often do you come here?	<u>Once</u> a week.
How many do you <u>want</u> ?	Just one, please.
Is this your sister?	No, my <u>friend</u> .
Aren't they the same?	No, they're <u>different</u> .
That's my coat!	No, it <u>isn't</u> .

6 Monitor the pronunciation of the final consonant clusters as students repeat the words.

7 Answers

The following are the most likely answers:

1. things you can eat or drink: toast, beans, orange, milk
2. things you can wear: belt, pants, shorts
3. parts of the body: waist, arm, hand, chest
4. animals: elephant, wasp, fox
5. people: adult, child, yourself, parent, boyfriend
6. ways people feel: pleased, amused, depressed, shocked, cold

8 One student from each pair should report back. Ask the first pair for *things you can eat or drink*, ask the second for *things you can wear*, and so on.

EXTENSION

For homework, ask students to collect three words that end in a consonant cluster (these could be taken from their course work, for example). These three words should have some connection (e.g., all found in the home). Discourage plurals, which often end in a consonant + -*s*. Students should report their words in class. Collect their answers and use them to do an activity similar to the one in **6** through **8** at a later time.

UNIT 21 Syllabic consonants; more on consonant clusters at the ends of words

BACKGROUND

Most syllables contain a vowel. In some words, though, like *middle* /ˈmɪdl/ and *listen* /ˈlɪsn/, the final syllable consists only of the last consonant. Consonants that form a syllable by themselves are referred to as *syllabic consonants*, and are sometimes written with a small line under the consonant – [l̩], [n̩]. The consonants /l/ and /n/ are by far the most common syllabic consonants in English. Syllabic consonants, the focus of tasks **1** to **5** in this unit, occur only in unstressed syllables. Note that although all the syllabic consonants practiced here are in the final syllable of a word, syllabic consonants can also occur in the middle of a word, as in *hospitalize* (with syllabic /l/) or *fattening* (with syllabic /n/).

1 Students may tend to insert a vowel sound between the last two consonants; however, native speakers normally would not.

Get students to stop after the /t/ or /d/ sound in one of the words in the first line, holding the tip of the tongue in place, and then to concentrate on saying /l/ without moving the tongue. Emphasize that the tip of the tongue should not move away from the tooth ridge (the rough ridge behind the upper front teeth) as they say the two consonants. Moving the tongue tip will cause a vowel sound to be added. (To feel the way the tongue moves from /d/ or /t/ to /l/, students could also practice slowly saying a word like *badly* or *quietly*.) Then have them practice with one of the words in the second line, for syllabic /n/.

BACKGROUND

In the words in the box in **1**, syllabic /l/ or /n/ follows a /t/ or /d/. When this happens, the tongue tip goes to the tooth ridge to produce the /t/ or /d/ and stays there without moving to make the /l/ or /n/. For syllabic /l/ (as in *bottle*), the tongue tip stays in place, and one or both sides of the tongue go down to let the air out laterally. Note that the /t/ before a syllabic /l/ is *voiced* in American and Canadian English, and sounds the same as a /d/; thus, a pair of words like *metal* and *medal* are pronounced the same way. (For more information on voicing /t/, see the notes for Unit 10.)

If syllabic /n/ follows a /d/ (as in *sudden*), the tongue tip stays at the tooth ridge and the buildup of air for the stop /d/ is released through the nose as the soft palate is lowered for /n/. If syllabic /n/ follows a /t/, the /t/ has a special pronunciation. The /t/ is usually either accompanied by or replaced by a glottal stop, which is made by pressing the vocal cords together to stop the air. (A glottal stop is the sound at the beginning of each syllable in *uh-oh*.)

2 Some students may tend to insert a full vowel sound between the last two consonants. You could point out that although the words end in a syllabic consonant, a *very short* vowel sound could be added before the last consonant in the words here (but not in the words in **1**). Correct students if they produce anything longer than a very short vowel sound here.

BACKGROUND

Instead of a syllabic consonant, it is possible to insert the vowel /ə/ in the words in the box in **2** (for example, *terrible* /ˈtɛrəbəl/ or *listen* /ˈlɪsən/). When native speakers do this, they pronounce this as a very short vowel. Learners of English often tend to make this vowel too long, and this should be discouraged.

3 Answers

1. A: Where's your ___cousin___ ?
   B: She's in the ___hospital___ .
   A: What's the matter?
   B: She fell off her ___bicycle___ .

2. A: Have you ___eaten___ ?
   B: No, I ___haven't___ .
   A: Would you like some ___chicken___ ?
   B: Just a ___little___ .

3. A: Press that ___button___ .
   B: This one in the ___middle___ ?
   A: Yes.
   B: What'll ___happen___ ?
   A: Just ___listen___ .

4. A: What's in this ___bottle___ ?
   B: A ___chemical___ .
   A: What's it for?
   B: Something ___special___ !

5. A: When's your math ___final___ ?
   B: At ___eleven___ .
   A: How do you feel?
   B: ___Terrible___ .

Note that students will not need to use all the words in the boxes in **1** and **2** to fill in the blanks.

6 Model the task. Students should interview a number of people and note how many people give each answer.

7 When reporting back, students can make statements such as these: *Most people I talked to liked science best in school, Nobody I spoke to wanted to be a politician.*
When students report back, monitor the pronunciation of the underlined parts of the words. These contain either syllabic consonants or consonant clusters.

UNIT 22
Groups of consonants in the middle of words; simplifying final consonant clusters

Groups of consonants in the middle of words

BACKGROUND

The consonant groups practiced here include both consonant clusters – two or more consonant sounds pronounced within one syllable without an intervening vowel (e.g., /ky/ in *secure* /sɪ'kyʊr/) – and sequences of consonants that are broken up between two syllables (e.g., /ks/ in *success* /sək'sɛs/).

1 Tell students to say the words aloud to each other to help them with the task. The consonant groups here are "hidden" ones, not immediately apparent from the spelling. For example, *x* in *taxi* is pronounced /ks/ even though it is only one consonant letter. And none of the words pronounced with /ky/ here is spelled with either *k* or *y*; in fact, the consonant sound /y/ is represented by a vowel letter (*u*) rather than a consonant.

Answers

/ks/	/ky/	/kw/
accident	occupation	require
success	secure	equal
taxi	particular	frequent
vaccination	calculator	liquid
accent		
exercise		

The words in the box not shown in the table are *record, account, occur*.

3 Answers

1. The letters   qu   are usually pronounced /kw/.
2. The letters *cc* are usually pronounced /ks/ before the letters   e   and   i .

Students may have trouble pronouncing the words in **1** either because they are confused about how the spellings in the words should be pronounced or because they have difficulty in pronouncing groups of consonants.

1. /ks/: Some students tend to drop the /k/ in /ks/. It might help simply to point out that the spellings *cc* and *x* in the first column each have two sounds /k/ and /s/. It might also help to show students how to break this consonant sequence up between two syllables – for example, AC-cent /'æk-sɛnt/.
2. /ky/: Students may not know when the letter *u* includes the sound /y/. See the next section, *Background*.
3. /kw/: Simply pointing out that the spelling *qu* is usually pronounced /kw/ may help. Note that for /kw/, the lips should be rounded when saying /k/, in preparation for /w/.

BACKGROUND

The spelling rules in the Student's Book do not cover all the words in the table. For example, no rules are given for the spelling *x* pronounced /ks/ or for the spellings that represent /ky/.

The letter *x* is usually pronounced /ks/. However, when it comes before a stressed vowel letter or before *h* + a stressed vowel letter, it is usually pronounced /gz/ (for example, *exact, example, executive, exist, exhausted, exhibit*). As "usually" suggests, there are exceptions; for example, *exile* and *exit* can be pronounced with /gz/ even though the following vowel is not stressed. Note that the combination *xc* is also pronounced /ks/ if it comes before *e* or *i* (e.g., *excellent, excited*).

The words with /ky/ in the table all contain the spelling *cu*. The rules for when to pronounce /y/ as part of a *u* spelling are somewhat complicated, but after the letter *c* (or *cc*), the letter *u* generally is pronounced with a /y/ sound unless (1) the consonant letter that follows is at the end of the word (as in *occur*) or (2) two (or more) consonant letters follow (as in *occurrence, cultivate,* or *cuddle*).

4 Point out that the *p* in *raspberries* is not pronounced.

To reinforce the spelling patterns practiced in **1** through **3**, you might ask students how the *x* in *taxi* and the *cc* in *successful* are pronounced (/ks/), and how the *qu* in *frequently* and *equipment* is pronounced (/kw/). You could also ask students to find words in the box that have the sound /y/ in the underlined part, reminding them that the sound /y/ isn't always spelled with the letter *y* (the words here are *computers, opinions, onions, popular*).

You could point out to more advanced students that many Americans and Canadians do not pronounce the /t/ in /nt/ before an unstressed vowel, as in the word *painting*.

5 Point out that what is shown within slashes on the left in the Student's Book represents sounds and not letters. So, for example, /zb/ in number 2 is not necessarily written with the letters *zb*. In doing this exercise, students have to decide which words in the box in **4** contain the sounds given (there are two words in each case) and which of these is appropriate in the context of the sentence in **5**. Alternatively, they may look for words that fit the context and decide which of these contains the required sound.

Answers

1. We need some new ___equipment___ for the office.
2. Have you met her new ___husband___?
3. It costs a lot nowadays to buy a good ___painting___.
4. Please play your records ___quietly___. The baby's asleep.
5. I took a ___taxi___ to the airport.
6. Her ___boyfriend___ brings her flowers every day.
7. I bought a pound of ___onions___.
8. She's studying to be a ___doctor___.
9. He's a very ___popular___ actor.
10. The price of the house did not include kitchen ___appliances___.

EXTENSION

Have students find the two words in the box in **4** that have each of the sounds shown on the left in **5** and write them in sets (e.g., *ta*x*i* – su*cc*essful).

Simplifying final consonant clusters

6 Nonnative speakers may be relieved to learn that even native speakers find some sequences of consonants difficult to pronounce and therefore often simplify them. Note that the generalization given in the Student's Book about -*s* and -*ed* endings not being omitted is an oversimplification, since the -*ed* ending (but not the -*s* ending) can be omitted in some environments (see *Background*, next section). Students need to be careful, though, about which consonants they leave out, especially when an ending like -*ed* is involved, to make sure that an omitted consonant does not sound like a grammar mistake. Students also need to understand that not all clusters can be simplified.

BACKGROUND

When speaking at normal speed, native speakers often completely or nearly omit one of the middle consonant sounds, especially /t/, /d/, /θ/, or (less often) /k/, when a sequence of three or more consonants occurs together at the end of a word or at a word boundary. This often happens in the following situations:

1. when /t/ or /θ/ is followed by /s/ and preceded by another fricative or /n/; for example, *costs, prints, fifths*
2. when /t/ or /d/ is followed by a word beginning with certain other consonants and the /t/ is preceded by /f/ or /s/ or the /d/ is preceded by /z/, /l/, or /n/; for example, *left quickly, last Saturday, used books, old pajamas, sand castle*
3. when /t/ or /d/ is preceded by another stop consonant or an affricate and followed by certain other consonants (especially other stops or affricates); for example, *kept going, looked nice, changed planes, changed jobs*

Omission can occur in some other contexts, too, as in *don't know*. In addition, the contexts where omission of a consonant occurs can differ from speaker to speaker. For a more detailed description of the contexts in which deletion, especially of /t/ or

/d/, is likely, see Mary S. Temperley's "Linking and Deletion in Final Consonant Clusters" in Morley (1987, pp. 63–82), in the list of recommended books in To the Teacher, and "The Articulatory Target for Final -s Clusters" in *TESOL Quarterly*, Vol. 17, No. 3, Sept. 1983.

Further information and practice on simplifications such as these can be found in Part 5.

7   Answers

1. It   costs   too much.
2. He   lifts   weights.
3. He   asked   her to marry him.
4. I   don't   know yet.
5. I don't think she   trusts   him.

6. How much is this   gold   bracelet?
7. Six   months .
8. Let's stop for some   fast   food.
9. Thanks, anyway. I'm   just   looking.
10. Can you come   next   Saturday?

8   During repetition, encourage students to make these simplifications: 1. cos~t~s; 2. lif~t~s; 3. as~k~ed; 4. don'~t~ know; 5. trus~t~s; 6. gol~d~ bracelet; 7. mon~th~s; 8. fas~t~ food; 9. jus~t~ looking; 10. nex~t~ Saturday.

9   Answers

1. A: Let's stop for some fast food.
   B: Let's go to a real restaurant for a change.
   A: It costs too much.
   B: That's all you think about – money.

2. A: How does he stay in such great shape?
   B: He lifts weights.
   A: Has he been doing that for long?
   B: Six months.

3. A: How much is this gold bracelet?
   B: Two hundred dollars.
   A: Thanks, anyway. I'm just looking.

4. A: He asked her to marry him.
   B: I don't think she'll accept.
   A: Why not?
   B: I don't think she trusts him.

5. A: Can you come next Saturday?
   B: I don't know yet.
   A: Please try.

PART 4 *Stress and rhythm*

INTRODUCTION

Aims and organization

In Part 4, students learn about syllables in words, the pronunciation of stressed and unstressed syllables, and the rhythm of spoken English.

Unit 23   Syllables and stress (introduces the idea of syllables, stressed syllables, and unstressed syllables)
Unit 24   Patterns of stress in words
Unit 25   More practice (stress in numbers, stress in noun compounds)
Unit 26   Pronouncing unstressed syllables
Unit 27   Predicting stress in words, including words with some common endings
Unit 28   Rhythm (strong forms and weak forms)
Unit 29   More on rhythm
Unit 30   Rhythm and moving stress (moving stress in longer words, with focus on nationalities and numbers)

General notes

A syllable can be described as a group of sounds that are pronounced together. Syllables always contain a vowel, except in the case of syllabic consonants (see the notes for Unit 21). The vowel in an English syllable may be preceded by one or more consonants and may be followed by one or more consonants.

When a word is said on its own, its syllables will be either stressed or unstressed. Here are some examples of words showing stressed (marked ○ over the vowel) and unstressed (marked ○) syllables:

Some words have two kinds of stressed syllable: a *primary* stressed syllable and one or more *secondary* stressed syllables. For example, in the three-syllable word *guarantee*, the last syllable has primary stress, the first has secondary stress, and the middle syllable is unstressed. In dictionaries, the primary and secondary stressed syllables are typically indicated in one of two ways: *guarantee* /gærən'tiy/ or *guarantee* (gar'ən tē').

In the Student's Book, students for the most part just practice the difference between stressed and unstressed syllables, without distinguishing the two kinds of stressed syllables. Only the syllable with primary stress is considered to be stressed; all other syllables, including those with secondary stress, are considered to be unstressed. This seems to be a useful simplification for students at this stage, with syllables having secondary stress simply pronounced with a full rather than reduced vowel. Also, secondary stressed syllables often have stress only when the word is said in isolation, not when it is used in a sentence. The importance of knowing about stress in words in speaking English is discussed more in the General Notes for Part 6.

The *rhythm* of English is largely created by the patterns of stressed and unstressed syllables as words are grouped into phrases and sentences. The fact that the pronunciation of certain words (like *to* or *and*) differs in their stressed and unstressed forms is also important in giving English its characteristic rhythm.

UNIT 23   Syllables and stress

1   This task introduces the idea that words can be divided into syllables. Have students tap out the syllables, using their fingers or a pencil on their desks or using their feet, to help in counting. Demonstrate this for students. You may also want to point out that each syllable usually has a vowel sound (except in the case of a syllabic consonant, as in the last syllable of *impossible*).

Answers

1. furniture 3	6. collect 2	11. impossible 4
2. brought 1	7. anybody 4	12. electricity 5
3. blackboard 2	8. please 1	13. rabbit 2
4. examination 5	9. police 2	14. directions 3
5. remember 3	10. grandmother 3	15. good-bye 2

3   This introduces the idea of stressed syllables in words. Tell students that in English words with more than one syllable, one syllable is stressed, or stands out. You could explain that the stressed syllable sounds louder and longer than the other syllables. To pronounce a word correctly, students must learn where the stress goes.

Demonstrate by saying the example words from the Student's Book (or other words that students know) and drawing a large circle over the stressed vowel and small circles over the other vowels. You can use a rubber band that you stretch to demonstrate the lengthening of the vowel in stressed syllables. To check that students have understood, write other words that students know on the board and say them. Have students tell you which syllable is stressed, and draw a large circle over the vowel in that syllable and small circles over the other vowels, or select students to come to the board to draw the circles.

BACKGROUND

Stressed syllables in English (at least in words said in isolation) are generally longer, louder, and pronounced at a higher pitch than other syllables, though these features are not always all present. Stressed syllables also have a clear, full vowel, while the vowel in unstressed syllables, which tend to be shorter in length, is often reduced to /ə/. The features that signal stress in other languages are often different; for example, pitch change alone may signal stress, or all syllables may have clear, full vowels.

In some languages, the stress pattern of a word is predictable, with stress always falling on the same syllable in a word (for example, the first syllable in Czech words). Stress is English is not predictable in this way, though there are rules that can help students decide where to put the stress. (A few of these rules are given in Unit 27.)

4 Answers

1. furniture
2. no circle needed
3. blackboard
4. examination
5. remember
6. collect
7. anybody
8. no circle needed
9. police
10. grandmother
11. impossible
12. electricity
13. rabbit
14. directions
15. good-bye

Although some words here (e.g., *examination*) may be considered to have two kinds of stressed syllable, a syllable with primary stress and one or more syllables with secondary stress, students are asked to mark only the syllable with primary stress (the main, or strongest, stress), with all other syllables being considered unstressed.

EXTENSION

If students share a language in which one syllable in a word is normally stressed, have them list a few multisyllabic words in that language and say where the stress is in each. If students share a language like Japanese in which syllables are often considered to carry equal stress, have them list some words and phrases in that language to show that stress operates differently from the way it does in English.

When you write down new words for students to copy and learn, mark the stress using large and small circles. Encourage students to learn the stress patterns when they study the words.

---

6 Answers

Moscow 2   Cairo 2   Tokyo 3
Madrid 2   Jakarta 3   Bogota 3

To check the answers, write the names of the cities on the board. Ask students to come to the front and draw circles over the syllables. You could also ask what countries these cities are in, and have students mark the stress in the country names with circles.

If any students are from the countries where these cities are located, you could ask them to say the name of the city in their native language. Ask other students to decide whether the stress is the same as in English or different.

EXTENSION

You could extend the activity in **6** and **7** by asking for more capital cities, giving the names in English if students don't know them. If you think it is appropriate for your students, use this opportunity to show that it is sometimes difficult to decide how many syllables a word has. For example, *Tokyo* when said slowly would probably have three syllables, "To-ky-o," but if said quickly may have only two, "To-kyo."

If students have multisyllabic names with stressed and unstressed syllables, write some of them on the board. Ask other students to come and draw large and small circles over the names to indicate stressed and unstressed syllables.

---

8 Answers

At seven fifteen. ⟨○ ₒ ₒ ○⟩

I'll be away that weekend. ⟨ₒ ○ ○ ₒ⟩

Have you ever been to Brazil? ⟨○ ₒ ₒ○⟩

Is the station far away? ⟨○ ₒ ₒ ○⟩

I was hoping to invite you. ⟨○ ₒ ₒ ○⟩

I'm a stranger here myself. ⟨○ ₒ ₒ○⟩

What time does the movie begin? ⟨○ ₒ ₒ ○⟩

I went to Rio in July. ⟨○ₒ ₒ○⟩

9

When students repeat, monitor stress on the two-syllable words.

10 Answers

What time does the movie begin?	At seven fifteen.
I was hoping to invite you.	I'll be away that weekend.
Is the station far away?	I'm a stranger here myself.
Have you ever been to Brazil?	I went to Rio in July.

UNIT 24 Patterns of stress in words

1 Answers

The odd one out in each line is as follows:

1. chicken (○ ₒ)
2. Japan (ₒ ○)
3. president (○ ₒₒ)
4. appointment (ₒ ○ ₒ)
5. supermarket (○ ₒₒₒ)

EXTENSION

You could help students figure out a simple rule that explains the stress in some of the words in **1**. Ask students what they notice about stress in the words *injection, competition, information,* and *immigration*. (The stressed syllable is the one before the *-ion* ending.) Most words that end with *-ion* have stress in this position, irrespective of stress in the base form (that is, the word without *-ion*). Demonstrate this with the following:

inject – injection   inform – information

compete – competition   immigrate – immigration

Ask students to collect more words ending with *-ion* and see if the rule works for these. There is more on stress in words ending in *-ion* and some other common endings in Unit 27.

3 Answers

1. economics 4	6. biology 4	11. Italian 3
2. Chinese 2	7. photographer 4	12. September 3
3. August 2	8. chemistry 3	13. July 2
4. accountant 3	9. diplomat 3	14. Russia 2
5. Morocco 3	10. Arabic 3	15. Germany 3

If students need help in counting syllables, tap the board or a desk once for each syllable, or ask students to tap out the syllables.

4 During repetition, monitor students' use of stress in the words. You can stretch a rubber band to show the lengthening of the vowel in the stressed syllable.

5 Answers

1. accountant	4. Italian
2. August	5. Morocco
3. biology	

EXTENSION

1. Ask students to find any other words in **3** that fit each conversation in **5** *in terms of meaning*, and to draw circles to show the stress pattern of that word. Here is an example:

A: What does she do?

B: She's a diplomat. / B: She's a photographer.

2. Write the word *biology* (from conversation 3 in **5**) on the board, with circles to show the stress pattern. Underline the ending *-ology* and ask students to name

other subjects with that ending (e.g., *psychology, anthropology, archaeology, geology*). Write the words on the board as they suggest them, and then have a student draw a large circle over the stressed syllable in each. You could add some words that students are *not* likely to know (e.g., *ethnology, climatology*) and ask students to predict where the stress would go (that is, in the first *o* in *–ology*).

UNIT 25 More practice: stress in numbers, stress in noun compounds

Stress in numbers

1 Answers

The answers are underlined:

1. The next train to arrive on this platform is the <u>10:14</u> to Boston.
2. I have a very old car. It can only go about <u>50</u> miles an hour.
3. We could meet in my office. It's number <u>13</u>.
4. My brother is 35, but his wife is <u>17</u>!
5. It's very good, and it only cost me <u>$1.80</u>.
6. The hotel cost <u>$90.00</u> a night.
7. I think she was born in <u>1916</u>.

To check the answers, write the pairs of numbers on the board and point to the one you hear as the students say their answers. That way you can check students' ability to produce as well as hear the distinction between the numbers.

If students have difficulty distinguishing between the numbers, point out the difference in stress between a pair of *-ty* and *-teen* numbers, for example:

forty and fourteen

Say the two numbers, and then write them on the board, drawing circles over the vowels to show stress. Notice that this difference in stress does not always occur, though; in sentence 7, both *nineteen* and *sixteen* are stressed on the first syllable. For more details, see *Background* under **2** below.

2 This gives students practice in hearing the difference between numbers that end in *-teen* and *-ty*. With more advanced students, you may want to point out differences in the way the *t* in the endings is pronounced (see *Background* below) as well as differences in stress.

BACKGROUND

Numbers that end in *-teen* and *-ty* differ in stress (main stress is on the last syllable of *-teen* numbers and on the first syllable of *-ty* numbers) when they are said by themselves or at the end of a phrase or sentence. When these numbers are immediately followed by another word in the same phrase, however, the difference in stress is likely to disappear because the stress in -*teen* numbers tends to shift to the first syllable, as illustrated in the difference between these two examples:

It's ten-fifteen.   *fifteen miles an hour*

The stress in -*teen* numbers also shifts when counting:

. . . thirteen, fourteen, fifteen, sixteen . . .

The same stress shift occurs when two -*teen* numbers are contrasted, as in this example:

I said fifteen, not sixteen.

There is more on this type of shifting stress in Unit 30.

In North American English, there is also a difference in the way *t* is pronounced in most of the -*teen* and -*ty* numbers. The *t* in -*teen* numbers is pronounced as a voiceless stop /t/ regardless of how these numbers are stressed. The /t/ in *thirty*, *forty*, and *eighty* is normally pronounced as a voiced flap or tap – like a quick /d/ sound (see Unit 10). The second *t* in *twenty* is usually dropped: *twenty*. Some people also drop the *t* in *seventy* and *ninety*, especially in rapid speech, though other speakers pronounce the *t* in these numbers as the sound /d/.

EXTENSION

For further practice on numbers that end in -*teen* and -*ty*, play Bingo. Write the numbers 13, 14, 15, 16, 17, 18, 19, 30, 40, 50, 60, 70, 80, and 90 on the board. Tell students to write down four of the numbers. Then say the numbers slowly at random. Keep a note of which ones you have said. Students should cross out the numbers they have written down as they hear you say them. When a student has crossed out all four numbers, he or she should shout Bingo! That person has then won the game – assuming he or she has heard you correctly, of course. Ask the winner to read out the four numbers while you check them. After a few games like this, ask a student to take on the role of "caller."

Stress in noun compounds

BACKGROUND

A noun compound is a combination of words – two nouns, or another kind of word plus a noun – that functions as a single noun. Notice that in some cases, a compound can have a new meaning (as in *blackboard*) that could not be easily predicted from the meaning of the parts. A noun compound can be written as one word, as two words, or with a hyphen. It is pronounced as a single word. The main stress is typically on the first word, for example:

hay fever

There are exceptions to this; for example, *scarlet fever* which has strong stress on both words:

scarlet fever

In noun compounds that have a single main stress on the first word, the second word can usually be considered to have secondary stress; the vowel that would be stressed when the word is said by itself usually remains a full vowel and is not reduced, though, again, there are exceptions (e.g., words like *policeman* in which *-man* is pronounced with unstressed /ə/). When two words are used together without forming a noun compound, they have ordinary phrasal stress, with strong stress on both words. Compare, for example, *a bluebird* (a noun compound referring to a particular kind of bird) and *a blue bird* (a phrase that could refer to any bird that is blue in color):

a bluebird (noun compound)   *a blue bird* (phrase)

6 Explain that the stress is usually different when two words come together to form a noun compound and when two words are used in an ordinary phrase. Give some examples that illustrate the differences between the two structures. For example, a *drugstore* (noun compound) is a particular kind of store where you can buy medicines and cosmetics, but *a small store* (phrase) describes any store that happens to be small in size:

a drugstore   *a small store*

Similarly, *a washing machine* (noun compound) is a special machine for washing clothes, but *an old machine* (phrase) could refer to any machine that is old:

a washing machine   *an old machine*

Answers

A		B	
1. a raincoat	☑	a wool coat	☐
2. a large office	☐	the post office	☑
3. a good driver	☐	a cab driver	☑
4. a long book	☐	a notebook	☑
5. a dining room	☑	a dirty room	☐
6. an office building	☑	a modern building	☐
7. a white house	☐	the White House	☑
8. a sleeping bag	☑	a sleeping child	☐

You could point out to more advanced students that the same sequence of words can sometimes be used either as a noun compound with a special meaning or as a phrase (e.g., a noun modified by an adjective); for example, *the White House* (a noun compound referring to the home of the president of the United States) versus *a white house* (any house that is white in color). Other examples of noun compounds like this are *greenhouse, blackboard, yellow jacket, and darkroom.*

7 Point out that when the first word has more than one syllable, the syllable with the main stress is the syllable that is stressed when that word is said by itself; for example:

living room   *alarm clock*   *shower curtain*

Answers

○ paintbrush
○ alarm clock
○ shower curtain
○ bookcase
○ desk lamp
○ orange juice
○ tomato sauce
○ can opener
○ lightbulbs

○ toothpaste
○ measuring tape
○ dish towels
○ cookbook
○ answering machine
○ frying pan
○ washing machine
○ garbage can
○ salad dressing

EXTENSION

Choose a few of the compound nouns in the list in **7** (for example, *paintbrush, desk lamp, cookbook*). Ask students to think of other compound nouns that have the same second word (e.g., *toothbrush, floor lamp, notebook*).

---

9 Discuss the names of any stores students may not be familiar with. Ask, for example, *What can you buy at a hardware store?*

During pairwork and reporting back, monitor students' use of noun compound stress on the store names as well as on the list of items in **7**.

EXTENSION

For **9**, ask students, *What are some other things Jennifer and Jason might need? Try to think of three more noun compounds. Where could they buy these things?*

---

10 Ask students if they have done any of these things recently and, if so, where they have done them.

EXTENSION

As a follow-up to **10**, ask students to work in pairs and add two more items to the list. They can use items from the shopping list in **7** or ones that they think of themselves. Each pair then asks the rest of the class about good places (or the best place, the nearest place, and so on) to buy or do these things. Make a note of any new noun compounds used in the questions or answers. Here are some possible additions to the list: *buy a newspaper/a notebook/a photo album/a wedding ring/a bathing suit/hiking boots/chopsticks; go for a day trip/go birdwatching.*

UNIT 26 Pronouncing unstressed syllables

1 Direct students' attention to the words in boxes A and B. Ask students, *What can you say about stress and the way the underlined vowels are pronounced in each pair of words?* Students should notice that the sound of the underlined vowel changes when it is not stressed. They might also note that in each pair of words, the unstressed vowel is shorter or has a less clear sound than the stressed vowel, or that the stressed vowels have several different sounds but the unstressed vowels all sound the same or very similar.

2 Tell students that the vowel /ə/ is very common in unstressed syllables in English (although it is not the *only* vowel found in unstressed syllables) and that it has the name *schwa* (pronounced /ʃwɑ/). It is useful to give the sound a name to make it easy to refer to.

[handwritten: reduced (weakened)]

Explain that this vowel is very short. In unstressed syllables, it does not have a clear sound. For English speakers, /ə/ is the vowel produced when the tongue is at rest, in a neutral position in the center of the mouth; the tongue is not pushed forward or pulled back. For more on the production of /ə/, see the notes for Units 2 and 3.

Point out that /ə/ can be spelled in many different ways.

BACKGROUND

A distinction can be made between full (or strong) vowels and reduced (or weak) vowels. All the vowels listed in the Key to phonetic symbols on page v can occur as full vowels. Stressed syllables always include a full vowel. Reduced vowels include /ə/ in *ago* and *mother*, /ɪ/ in *music* or *active*, and the vowels in *happy* and *situation* that are sometimes represented by the symbols /i/ and /u/ respectively. Unstressed syllables may include a full vowel or any of the reduced vowels, although the reduced vowel /ə/ is the most common vowel in unstressed syllables.

In many words, an unstressed vowel can be pronounced as either /ə/ or /ɪ/ without too much difference; for example, you can pronounce *boxes* as /ˈbɑxəz/ or /ˈbɑxɪz/ and *women* as /ˈwɪmən/ or /ˈwɪmɪn/. Often, it doesn't matter whether you say /ə/ or /ɪ/ in an unstressed syllable as long as you make the vowel very short.

Note that /ə/ can be spelled with any vowel letter and many combinations of vowel letters.

[handwritten in right margin: may use for function word - reduction + explanation]

3 Answers

1. c<u>o</u>mpletely
2. jeal<u>ous</u>
3. <u>a</u>part<u>me</u>nt
4. bi<u>o</u>logy
5. excell<u>e</u>nt
6. m<u>a</u>chine
7. wom<u>a</u>n
8. wom<u>e</u>n
9. s<u>u</u>cc<u>e</u>ss
10. dist<u>a</u>nce
11. v<u>a</u>n<u>i</u>lla
12. quest<u>io</u>n

EXTENSION

On the board, write words from **2** and **3** that have common endings pronounced with the vowel /ə/, and underline the endings: *fam<u>ous</u>, jeal<u>ous</u>; instru<u>ment</u>, apart<u>ment</u>; dist<u>ance</u>; sugges<u>tion</u>, ques<u>tion</u>; excell<u>ent</u>.* Point out or elicit from students that these endings are pronounced with the vowel /ə/. Ask students to think of more words with each of these endings (e.g., *nervous, dangerous, curious, serious, delicious; department, experiment, government, argument, development; performance, appearance, entrance, attendance; information, education, discussion, opinion; silent, absent, violent*). Note that some words ending in *-ance* or *-ent* will have a syllabic consonant rather than /ə/ (e.g., *importance, student*).

4 During repetition, monitor students' use of stress and their pronunciation of /ə/. Point out that all the underlined vowels in **3** are pronounced (more or less) the same way, as /ə/. For example, note that the second syllables of *woman* and *women* are pronounced the same even though they are spelled differently.

To check that they are not using full vowels in place of /ə/, students can practice at home in front of a mirror. For example, students can make sure that they do not pronounce the *o* in *c<u>o</u>mpletely* with rounded lips (as for /ow/) or open their mouths wide for the *a* in *m<u>a</u>chine* (as for /ɑ/).

Make sure that students do not say the unstressed syllables *too* quickly, shortening them *too* much; this can make the syllables sound as if they were dropped. If students rush through the unstressed syllables, simply telling them to slow down should help.

5 Tell students that /ər/ is very common in unstressed syllables where the vowel letter is followed by the letter *r*. Remind students that when /r/ comes after /ə/, it changes the way /ə/ sounds, and that /ər/ is pronounced together as a single sound. (For more information on the production of /ər/, see the notes for Unit 8.)

If necessary, remind students that the underlined parts of the words here are all pronounced the same, even if they are spelled differently. Students should not, for example, round their lips for the underlined sounds in *visit<u>or</u>* or *pict<u>ure</u>* (as they would for the sounds /ɔ/ or /uw/) or open their mouths wide for the underlined sound in *doll<u>ar</u>* (as they would for /ɑ/).

6 Model the task. One student says a word in the box; the other student says a word in the box that has the opposite meaning. Students can draw lines to connect the pairs of opposites.

Answers

The following are the most likely answers:

higher and lower	richer and poorer
younger and older	longer and shorter
faster and slower	sooner and later
hotter and colder	harder and softer
under and over	thicker and thinner
lighter and darker	

8 During repetition, monitor students' use of stress and their pronunciation of /ə/ and /ər/.

9 If necessary, explain the meaning of *challenging* before students work in pairs. A job that is challenging tests your abilities and requires that you work hard; it is both difficult and interesting.

EXTENSION

Ask other questions about the pairs of jobs in **9**, such as *Which job is more stressful?, Which job is more interesting?, Which job requires more education?* Or, you could add other pairs of jobs; for example: *lawyer/college professor, air traffic controller/dentist, dancer/taxi driver.*

UNIT 27 Predicting stress in words

1 Explain that although word stress in English is not fixed – that is, it does not go on the same syllable in every word – it is possible to see some general patterns. Understanding these can help students predict where stress goes in new words they meet.

If necessary, review the meaning of *noun, verb,* and *adjective.*

Answers

carry V	famous A	daughter N	husband N
forget V	careful A	modern A	prefer V
frighten V	kitchen N	friendly A	doctor N

2 Answers

◯ o	◯ o	◯ o	◯ o
carry	famous	daughter	husband
o ◯	◯ o	◯ o	o◯
forget	careful	modern	prefer
◯ o	◯ o	◯ o	◯ o
frighten	kitchen	friendly	doctor

3 Answers

Most __nouns__ and __adjectives__ are stressed on the first syllable.
Some __verbs__ are stressed on the first syllable, and others on the second.

EXTENSION

Teach noun-verb pairs in which the noun is stressed on the first syllable and the verb on the second syllable. These include:

record/record   insult/insult   conduct/conduct

suspect/suspect   present/present   permit/permit

Write one of these pairs, marking stress with circles, on the board. Tell students that one word is a noun and the other a verb. Using the rule in **3**, ask students to figure out which is a noun and which is a verb and then say the pair. Say other words from these pairs and ask students whether you are saying a noun or a verb. Then have students work in pairs to fill in the blanks in sentences with the correct (noun or verb) form, marking stress on the word with big and small circles; for example, *The airline had an excellent safety _____.*

4 Answers

1. decision
2. suggestion
3. institution
4. identification
5. equality
6. possibility
7. responsibility
8. personality
9. magnetic
10. scientific
11. enthusiastic
12. democratic
13. musical
14. medical
15. political
16. psychological

Many of the longer words here have two kinds of stressed syllable, a primary stressed syllable and a secondary stressed syllable; for example, ˌinsti'tution, iˌdentifi'cation, ˌpossi'bility, reˌsponsi'bility. Students mark only the primary (main) stress. (For more about this distinction, see General Notes for Part 4).

5 Answers

1. invention
2. examination
3. ability
4. opportunity
5. electronic
6. romantic
7. practical
8. physical

6 Answer

Words that end in *-ion, -ity, -ic,* and *-ical* usually have the main stress on the syllable <u>before</u> the ending.

EXTENSION

You could give students additional words that end in *-ion, -ity, -ic,* and *-ical,* some of which do and some of which do not follow the rule given in **6**. Ask students whether each word follows the rule or not. Some common exceptions include *arithmetic, Arabic, Catholic, lunatic; television, intersection, dandelion.*

---

7 Answers

The following are some possible answers:

You might say:	but probably not:
a romantic question	romantic ability
a fantastic opportunity	a fantastic examination
a scientific discussion	a scientific composition
physical ability	a physical invention
a musical composition	a musical question
a medical examination, the medical profession	a medical personality
an electronic invention	an electronic suggestion
an enthusiastic personality	an enthusiastic opportunity
a political discussion	a political profession
a practical suggestion	a practical opportunity

This task is a challenging one. Some words tend not to occur together because of their meanings, while others simply do not sound as natural as other combinations.

8 Note that most, but not all, of the words have the endings practiced in **4** through **7**. The words *pleasant, humor,* and *patience* follow the rules for two-syllable adjectives and nouns presented in **1** through **3**.

9 Students should work in groups of three or four to discuss their ideas. They can then report to the rest of the class. You might also ask students which qualities they think are the *least* important in a friend, husband or wife, and so on.

UNIT 28 Rhythm

BACKGROUND

A number of common words (grammar words) have two pronunciations, sometimes called their *strong* and *weak* forms. The strong, or stressed, forms are used when the words are given special emphasis or said on their own or in final position, and the weak forms are used on other occasions. These words are normally unstressed and said with their weak forms. This plays an important role in giving English its characteristic rhythm. The weak forms of most of these words include the vowel sound /ə/.

Words with weak forms that contain /ə/ include the following: *a, am, an, and, are, as, at, but, can, could, do, does, for, from, had, has, have, her, must, of, should, some, than, that, the, them, there, to, us, was, were,* and *would.* (Note that some of these words also may have weak forms without /ə/; for example, *and* can be pronounced as a syllabic consonant /n/.) Many learners tend to use the strong forms of these words where native speakers of English would use the weak forms. Therefore, for most students the tasks in this unit, which concentrates on the weak forms of just three of these words – *to, and,* and *for* – will be useful. More practice of strong and weak forms can be found in Part 7.

2 Students should read over the sentences before listening to the recording to help them predict which word they will hear. You could point out that although weak forms may be hard to hear, they can often be predicted from the context.

Answers

1. What's __for__ dinner?
2. I'll go __and__ see.
3. I have nothing __to__ say.
4. A hundred __and__ forty.
5. I'm going __to__ Florida.
6. I have __to__ go.

7. It's __for__ you.
8. Two __for__ a dollar.
9. My mother __and__ father.
10. I have a lot __to__ do.
11. Not __for__ long.
12. What's six __and__ eight?

4 Answers

The following are the most likely answers:

1. bread and __butter__
2. bacon and __eggs__
3. cheese and __crackers__
4. lettuce and __tomatoes__
5. peanut butter and __jelly__

6 This is an "around-the-class" activity. Explain that each student has to try to outdo the previous one in the amount he or she is going to eat. Have students practice first by using the example conversation in their books. Student A says, *I'm really hungry. When I get home I'm going to have some bacon and eggs.* Student B then tops that by saying, *I'm going to have bacon and eggs, and bread and butter.* Student C adds *lettuce and tomatoes.* Student D adds another item from **4**. Student E finishes with the final item; for example, *I'm going to have bacon and eggs, bread and butter, lettuce and tomatoes, peanut butter and jelly, and cheese and crackers.* Do this once or twice with different students, encouraging them to speak fluently without long hesitations and to use the weak form of *and*.

Then ask each student to think of another food combination. Encourage them to be imaginative (e.g., cornflakes and peas, spaghetti and mustard). Then repeat the around-the-class activity using their own food combinations rather than the ones in **4**. Stop each round when there are five or six items on the menu. For the first few rounds, write each new food combination on the board as it is added to help students remember. Then, if it doesn't interfere too much with fluency, do a few rounds in which students have to remember what other students have said up to that point and add a food combination themselves.

Here are some more conventional combinations if students run out of ideas: rice and beans, ham and eggs, coffee and cake, hamburger and french fries (or burger and fries), chips and salsa, meat and potatoes, fish and chips, milk and cookies, spaghetti and meatballs.

UNIT 29 More on rhythm

BACKGROUND

The term *rhythm* here refers to the patterns of stressed and unstressed syllables that are found in a sentence. Stressed syllables can follow one another, as in the following:

Please come.

Or they may be separated by intervening unstressed syllables, as in the examples in **1** in the Student's Book.

So far, the term *stress* has been used to refer to the stressed syllable in individual words or stressed syllables in short phrases. When a word or phrase is used in a sentence, however, these syllables may or may not be stressed. This reflects a difference between what is often referred to as "word stress" vs. "sentence stress" or "prominence." This is discussed further in Part 6.

1 Tap out the rhythm of each sentence. If necessary, point out that stressed syllables are longer (that is, take longer to say) than unstressed syllables.

2, 3 Answers

What did she say? 2	Milk and bread. 1
I hope you can come. 3	I'll call the police. 3
What do we need? 2	She told me to rest. 3
Here's your change. 1	Out to lunch. 1
Where'd he go? 1	So do I. 1
Give me your purse. 2	Thanks very much. 2

Students here practice some common rhythmic patterns of English, in which stressed syllables are separated by one or two unstressed syllables. Note that students will need to be aware of the number of syllables in each sentence in order to decide whether it follows pattern 1, 2, or 3.

Refer back to the sentences in **1** if students have difficulty. At the end, you could have students say first all the sentences following pattern 1, then all the sentences following pattern 2, and finally all those following pattern 3.

4 Answers

A: What did she say?
B: She told me to rest.

A: Here's your change.
B: Thanks very much.

A: I hope you can come.
B: So do I.

A: Where'd he go?
B: Out to lunch.

A: What do we need?
B: Milk and bread.

A: Give me your purse.
B: I'll call the police.

If students come up with any mismatched conversations, give a hint as to the correct answer by telling them which pattern of rhythm it follows.

EXTENSION

While checking the answers in **4**, ask students questions about the conversations. For example, *Who might be talking?*, *What are they talking about?*, *Where are they talking?*

5 In these dialogs, a fairly regular pattern of rhythm is established and repeated. In each dialog, the rhythm is slightly different, with a different number of unstressed syllables between or following the stressed syllables. Note that words that are said by one speaker and then repeated by the other (e.g., *Thursday, Friday,* and *Saturday,* in the first dialog) are usually not stressed when they are repeated. There is more on this in Unit 39.

To establish the pattern of rhythm in each dialog, it can be helpful for students to tap out the rhythm (or clap) as you read the dialog aloud.

After students practice in pairs, call on a few pairs to perform their continuations of the dialogs. Other students can tap or clap to reinforce the rhythmic pattern.

EXTENSION

Songs and poems often have similar repeated patterns of rhythm. For more practice with rhythm, choose one to practice with your students, marking the stressed syllables. Or consult Carolyn Graham's books of jazz chants – *Jazz Chants* (Oxford University Press, 1979) and *Small Talk* (Oxford University Press, 1986) – for ideas. Rap music is another source you might investigate.

UNIT 30   Rhythm and moving stress

BACKGROUND

Many words have both a syllable with primary stress and a syllable with secondary stress that occurs earlier in the word, for example: ˌJapaˈnese. When these words are used in connected speech before another word (rather than on their own or at the end of a phrase or sentence), the main stress frequently shifts to what ordinarily is the secondary stressed syllable. For example: a ˈJapanese ˈartist. This is sometimes referred to as *stress shift*. Stress shift happens particularly when the word is immediately followed by another stressed syllable. In the phrase *a Japanese electrician*, the stress is more likely to remain on the last syllable: a ˌJapaˈnese elecˈtrician. Although stress shift can occur in any word with both primary and secondary stress, it most often happens in adjectives.

1 Listening script

A: Do you want to see a picture of the English class I've been teaching?
B: Hmm. That's a good picture. They look like a pretty mixed group of students.
A: Yeah, it's a very mixed group. They're all from different countries – mostly European and Asian, though.
B: So where are they all from?
A: Well, you've met Tomo, right?
B: Yes, he was at the party, wasn't he?
A: Right. He's a doctor. He's Japanese. Well, you can see him at the back on the right.
B: Oh, yeah, I recognize him.
A: And the other three students along the back are a journalist – she's Polish. That's the one next to Tomo.
B: Uh-huh.
A: And then next to her is a dentist. She's Chinese.
B: They seem to have a lot of different jobs.
A: The variety is amazing. At the back on the left is a diplomat. She's Spanish. Pretty important, too, I think.
B: Really?
A: Then next to her is a businessperson. He's Taiwanese. Then at the front on the left is a teacher. He's Colombian.
B: And then who are the two on the other side of Tomo?
A: Well, the woman next to Tomo is an actor. She's Italian. And then at the front next to her is a farmer. He's Vietnamese.

Answers

dentist: Chinese
diplomat: Spanish
businessperson: Taiwanese
teacher: Colombian

journalist: Polish
doctor: Japanese
actor: Italian
farmer: Vietnamese

2 Answers

    ○   ○   ○   ○
Japanese   Chinese   Taiwanese   Italian

○   ○   ○   ○
Polish   Spanish   Colombian   Vietnamese

Although students are asked to mark only the syllable with the main (or primary) stress, note that some of these words also have a syllable with secondary stress: ˌJapaˈnese, ˌTaiwaˈnese, ˌVietnaˈmese.

4 Explain that in some words in English, particularly longer words, there is some-times a difference between stress when the word is said on its own and when it is said in a context. If this happens, stress always moves to an earlier syllable in the word. In the nationalities given here, for example, stress can move away from the last syllable to the first syllable in the word if another stressed syllable immediately follows the word.

Ask students to look at the example given in the Student's Book:

      ◯   ◯   ◯

He's Japanese.   but   He's a Japanese doctor.

You can explain the moving stress by saying that the stress on *doc-* pushes the stress on *-nese* away from it to an earlier syllable. In English rhythm, stressed syllables typically alternate with unstressed syllables rather than being next to each other.

Listening script

Note: The syllables with primary stress are in bold type.

1. He's **Ja**panese. He's a **Jap**anese **doc**tor.
2. She's **Pol**ish. She's a **Pol**ish **jour**nalist.
3. She's Chi**nese**. She's a **Chi**nese **den**tist.
4. She's **Span**ish. She's a **Span**ish **dip**lomat.
5. He's Taiwa**nese**. He's a **Tai**wanese **bus**inessperson.
6. He's Co**lom**bian. He's a Co**lom**bian **tea**cher.
7. She's I**tal**ian. She's an I**tal**ian **ac**tor.
8. He's Vietna**mese**. He's a **Viet**namese **farm**er.

Answers

1. Japanese	☑	5. Taiwanese	☑
2. Polish	☐	6. Colombian	☐
3. Chinese	☑	7. Italian	☐
4. Spanish	☐	8. Vietnamese	☑

EXTENSION

If students are adults with occupations and varying nationalities, have them describe one another using this pattern: *That's Tomo. He's a Japanese doctor.* They should use moving stress where appropriate.

---

5 Explain that for some numbers, too, stress can move. The main stress may be on the last syllable when the number is said on its own or at the end of a sentence, but the stress can shift to an earlier syllable when the number is said in context, particularly when another stressed syllable immediately follows it.

7 Tell students to look at the pictures. Ask them questions like these: *Where does Emma live?, What number does Manuel live at?, What's Julia's address?* Students should answer as in the conversations in **5**. Correct them when stress placement is wrong. Students then work in pairs to make similar conversations.

INTRODUCTION

Aims and organization

This section presents and practices differences between the pronunciation of words and phrases when they are said in isolation or at a slow speed (as they often are in the classroom), and when they are said in connected speech. In connected speech, words generally flow together and are spoken at a speed that many learners consider very fast.

Unit 31	Slow speech and connected speech (understanding sentences spoken at normal speed)
Unit 32	Common words and phrases in connected speech (weak forms; blended forms with *to*)
Unit 33	Linking words together: consonant + vowel (linking words that end with a consonant with words that begin with a vowel)
Unit 34	Linking words together: consonant + consonant (linking words that end with a consonant with words that begin with a different consonant)
Unit 35	More on linking words together with consonants (linking words that end and begin with the same consonant; assimilation of one consonant sound to resemble another; palatalization)
Unit 36	Sounds that link words: /w/ and /y/
Unit 37	Short sounds and disappearing /h/ (unstressed /ə/ at the beginning of a word and silent *h* in connected speech)

General notes

Before starting the units in Part 5, you might find it useful to explain to students that the features of pronunciation they are going to hear and practice are *not* features of very fast speech or of "lazy" speech. They are found in the normal conversational speech of native speakers of North American English (and native speakers with many other accents, too). By studying these aspects of pronunciation, students should find it easier to understand connected speech.

The emphasis in this section is often on *listening* to the differences between the pronunciation of slow speech and connected speech, rather than on having students produce these differences in their own speech. To sound like native speakers of English, learners will have to incorporate these features of pronunciation into their speech, but if they don't, they can still make themselves easily understood.

UNIT 31 Slow speech and connected speech

In Units 31 and 32, students are encouraged to make use of contextual clues to complete the tasks and, more generally, to help them make sense of connected speech.

1 Answers

1. It's over there.
2. There were five of them.
3. Ten after seven.
4. Can't you do it?
5. As soon as I can.
6. I don't think so.
7. Yeah, it's pretty good.
8. I have a bad cold.
9. I thought you said no.
10. I'll try to do it tomorrow.

These sentences contain examples of many of the features practiced later in Part 5: linking consonant to vowel (*ten after*), linking consonant to consonant (*don't think so*), linking and blending consonants (for example, /tʃ/ in *thought you*), and sounds that link vowel to vowel (for example, /w/ in *do it*). Also note that many of the words in these sentences are said with their weak forms; weak forms are dealt with in Unit 32 and, in more detail, in the units in Part 7.

2 Listening script

1. A: Have you seen my briefcase?
   B: It's over there.
2. A: How many men were in the car?
   B: There were five of them.
3. A: What time is it?
   B: Ten after seven.
4. A: Can you help me open this package?
   B: Can't you do it?
5. A: When will you be home?
   B: As soon as I can.
6. A: Excuse me, is this seat taken?
   B: I don't think so.
7. A: Have you read this book?
   B: Yeah, it's pretty good.
8. A: You don't look well.
   B: I have a bad cold.
9. A: Well, are we going to the movies?
   B: I thought you said no.
10. A: When are you going to clean the car?
    B: I'll try to do it tomorrow.

EXTENSION

Students could work in pairs and write their own short conversations with the sentences in **1** as the second line. You would probably want to limit the number of sentences they work with, for example, to three sentences. Then have students perform their conversations for the class. Encourage them to say their conversations at normal conversational speed.

---

3 Students should read all the answers in the balloons before listening to the recording. You may also want to have them try predicting the question that might be asked in each conversation.

Listening script

1. Have you been here long?
2. What do you have there?
3. Do you know him?
4. Do you come here often?
5. What's the matter?
6. Where are you going?
7. Are you ready to order?
8. What do you do?

Answers

a. 8	b. 2	c. 4
d. 1	e. 6	f. 5
g. 3	h. 7	

4 Answers

a. What do you do?
b. What do you have there?
c. Do you come here often?
d. Have you been here long?

e. Where are you going?
f. What's the matter?
g. Do you know him?
h. Are you ready to order?

6 Encourage students to say the conversations at normal speed. If necessary, use respellings to help with the pronunciations used in connected speech; for example "Whaddaya" (for *What do you*).

EXTENSION

As a further awareness activity for students, play a very short extract from any recording you have of English spoken at conversational speed by native speakers. Students should try to write down what is being said. Play the recording as many times as necessary. If appropriate, ask students to consider how this conversational English differs from the slow, careful English they may be used to hearing in the classroom – or that they produce themselves.

UNIT 32 Common words and phrases in connected speech

1 Students can work alone or in pairs to decide on possible answers. One word is missing from each space. Ask for suggestions for all the sentences before students listen to the recording.

Answers

1. Two _or_ three.
2. Call _an_ ambulance.
3. On _and_ off.
4. Saturday _or_ Sunday.
5. Some _are_ over here.

6. It's a container _of_ ice cream.
7. _Are_ they coming?
8. Is that a picture _of_ your sister?
9. He wants _a_ computer.
10. Some _have_ already paid.

2 During repetition, monitor the pronunciation of *or, an, and, are, of, a,* and *have.* Offer correction if these words are not pronounced with the unstressed sound /ə/ (schwa).

It is important not to emphasize these words or emphasize the sound /ə/ when you try to show, during correction, how they should be pronounced. The words should be said quickly and with their *weak* – not *strong* – forms (that is, with unstressed /ə/ and not a full vowel like /æ/ or /ɔ/; see **Background** in Unit 28 for more information on this). One simple way to avoid giving them emphasis is to be sure to say them in a sentence or phrase, as in the contexts given here, rather than isolating the words and saying them on their own.

3 Answer

Before a word that begins with a consonant sound, *of* is often pronounced /ə/. Before a word that begins with a vowel sound, *of* is usually pronounced /əv/.

Note that the word *and,* which appears in the last line of the table, can also be pronounced as a syllabic consonant /n/ (as in *hot and cold*).

4 Answers

1. want to
2. got to
3. Because
4. going to get you; going to meet you
5. You've got to teach them about

Point out that the types of informal spellings underlined in the Student's Book are used to show how the words sound. They may be used, for example, in writing the words of popular songs or in novels to show that people are speaking informally. They are not used in formal or academic writing.

EXTENSION

Look at the words of current pop songs that your students are familiar with for other examples of how connected speech is shown in written English. Examples can often be found in comic strips, too.

---

5 Answers

1. A: I've got to go now.
   B: OK. See you later.

2. A: What do you want to do?
   B: I don't know.

3. A: Did you see them?
   B: No. When were they here?

4. A: Can I get you anything?
   B: No, thanks.

5. A: Sorry about that.
   B: That's all right.

6. A: Are you going to go?
   B: I can't. I have to work late.

The missing parts include common phrases and common types of reduction that occur in informal conversation. The types of reduction include blended forms like *want to* and *going to* (practiced in more detail in **7** through **9** in this unit) and *did you* and *get you* (practiced in Unit 35, **7** through **9**) and weak forms of verbs and pronouns (practiced in Units 46, 47, and 48). Also note that the *ll* in *all right* is often not pronounced.

7   Note that the respellings given in parentheses (*gotta, wanna,* and so on) are, like the spellings in **4**, used to show how the words sound. Students should not use these in their own writing.

Other common blended forms with *to* include *used to* ("useta"), *ought to* ("oughta"), and *supposed to* ("supposeta").

8   This is an "around-the-class" activity. Have students practice first using the example conversation in their books. Student E (and any following students) should add a new excuse. Do this once or twice with different students to get students comfortable with the pattern.

Then ask each student to think of another excuse and repeat the around-the-class conversation using their own excuses. For the first few rounds, write each new excuse on the board as it is added to help students remember it. Then do a few rounds in which students have to remember what other students have said up to that point and add an excuse themselves. Alternatively, you could ask for suggestions first and make a list on the board of some likely excuses (for example, study for a test/walk the dog/babysit/go to the doctor/go shopping/pick up the kids from school). At the end, you could ask what the best excuse was or which excuses students use themselves.

Encourage students to use the blended forms shown in **7**. Although it is not necessary for students to incorporate these pronunciations in their own speech – and, indeed, use of these forms may sound unnatural if a person's speech is otherwise slow or not very fluent – it is important for students to be able to interpret these forms quickly in order to understand the conversational speech of native speakers. Getting some practice in saying the forms should help them with this.

EXTENSION

As a follow-up activity to **8** and **9**, have students make plans (real or imaginary) to do something together as a class. They should try to find a time when most class members can go. Information from the activity in **9** could help them decide when the greatest number of people would be free.

UNIT 33

Linking words together: consonant + vowel

When explaining the purpose of this unit, point out that the links are between a consonant *sound* at the end of a word with a following vowel *sound*. Some words end with a vowel *letter* but with a consonant *sound*, and some students may find this confusing. Explain this with a few examples. For example, write the words *one, these,* and *while* on the board. Ask whether the final letter of each is a vowel or consonant. Then ask whether the final sound in each is a vowel or consonant.

BACKGROUND

A common problem when listening to a new language is deciding where words begin and end. Students may expect words to be separated in speech as they are in writing, but in spoken English, words flow together. Native speakers generally link words within a phrase or thought group, pronouncing the words as if they were all run together, with no pauses corresponding to the spaces shown in writing. When linking a consonant and a following vowel, for example, speakers do not interrupt the breath to insert a glottal stop. Students may have problems understanding connected speech if they are not aware of the linking that occurs, both because of difficulties in determining word boundaries and because word-final sounds may undergo changes when linked to a following sound (such as the changes practiced in Unit 35). More obviously, failure to link words can make the speech of nonnative speakers often sound choppy. Note that in practicing linking, students will need to focus on the end of words – the part they are frequently inclined to drop.

The linking of consonant to vowel happens both (1) in cases where the final consonant in the first word follows a vowel (for example, *this afternoon*) and (2) those where the final consonant in the first word is part of a consonant cluster (for example, *found it*).

1. When the final consonant follows a vowel, it is usually pronounced as a medial consonant (one occurring in the middle of a word). Notice, for example, that /t/ is pronounced as a voiced flap in this situation, as in a *lot of* or *get up* – the same pronunciation it has in *city* or *letter* (for more on this pronunciation of /t/, see Unit 10).
2. When the final consonant is part of a consonant cluster, the consonant is often pronounced as if it were part of the following word, and the linking helps to break up and simplify the cluster: "foun dit," "lef tout." Notice, though, that the consonant that is moved over is weakly released, so that, for example, a voiceless stop (as in "lef tout") is not aspirated the way it would normally be at the beginning of a word (as in *too*; see Unit 9).

1 Answers

The consonant sounds that are linked to a following vowel are shown below:

1. An hour and a half.
   n   r   n
2. It's upstairs.
   s
3. He's an actor.
   z   n
4. I found it.
   d
5. Just a little.
   t

6. Neither am I.
   r   m
7. Both of us.
   θ   v
8. A while ago.
   l
9. That's a lot of money.
   s   t
10. This afternoon at four o'clock.
    s   n   r

Encourage students to speak without any gap between the words marked. Explain that English is not pronounced one word at a time, and model the linking shown. Writing some of the sentences with the words all run together can help demonstrate how the sentences should sound. It can also be helpful for students to slow down at first to concentrate on linking the words smoothly before saying the sentences at normal speed.

Sometimes students insert a glottal stop, in which the breath is stopped by pressing the vocal cords together, before the vowel at the beginning of any word. Discourage them from doing this between the linked words. Showing the consonant sound at the beginning of the second word can help: "it supstairs." Students also sometimes drop final consonants (especially /r/, /l/, and /n/ sounds); make sure that they pronounce these sounds and link them to the vowel that follows.

In the first sentence, note that the *h* in *hour* is silent; since this word begins with a vowel sound, it is preceded by *an* rather than *a*. Also note that *and* is pronounced with its weak form /ən/ (see Unit 28).

EXTENSION

Do one or both of the following activities to give students more practice with linking.

1. Choose some sentences from other course work. Have students draw linking marks to connect final consonant sounds to following vowel sounds. Students then practice saying the sentences, perhaps recording them on tape for you or other students to hear.
2. Choose some phrases or short sentences, for example, from other textbooks. Write these with the words in each thought group all run together. Point out that this is the way the sentences would be said. Students work in pairs and try to figure out where the words begin and end.

---

3 Ask some pairs of students to say their conversations to the rest of the class. Other students should monitor their pronunciation, checking to make sure that the pairs link consonants and vowels.

4 Answers

The following are the most likely answers:

a bottle of perfume
a pair of earrings
a box of candy
a bunch of flowers

a set of dishes
a book of jokes
a deck of cards
a roll of film

5 In monitoring pronunciation, check that the word *of* is pronounced /əv/ or /ə/ as well as that consonants and vowels are linked together. Note that there are two links in a *pair of earrings*. Also note that native speakers would pronounce *a set of dishes* with a flap /t/ in *set*.

7 Answers

The following are possible answers:

1. You put on   your coat/your clothes.
2. You put out   a fire.
3. You put away   your coat/your clothes.
4. You take off   your coat/your clothes.
5. You take out   the garbage/your coat.
6. You turn off   the radio/the stove/a light.
7. You turn up   the radio.
8. You get on   a bus.
9. You get in   a car.
10. You fill out   an application.

Note that when the final /t/ is linked to the following vowel in *put on, put out, get on,* and so on, the /t/ is pronounced as a voiced flap. See *Background*, at the beginning of this unit, as well as Unit 10.

UNIT 34   Linking words together: consonant + consonant

BACKGROUND

Nonnative speakers often have difficulty connecting a word that ends with a consonant sound with a following word that begins with a consonant sound. Some learners tend to insert a vowel between the words. Others may tend to drop one of the consonants, usually the consonant at the end of the first word. Although there are cases where deletion of a consonant is perfectly acceptable (e.g., in *last Saturday*), this strategy works in relatively few contexts. (More information on this is given in the teacher's notes for Unit 22, **6**.) This unit focuses chiefly on consonant sequences in which all the consonants are pronounced.

1 Answers

arrival — handed
drug — music
classical — time
left — store

truck — towel
orange — juice
dish — television
portable — driver

2   If students fail to link the consonant sounds at the word boundaries, rewrite the words to show the linking: "arriva ltime," "dru gstore," etc. Make sure that students do not add a vowel sound between the linked consonants. Students should also be discouraged from separately releasing the first of the linked consonants in *drugstore, left-handed,* and *truck driver* before pronouncing the following consonant. Note, however, that the two /ʤ/ sounds in *orange juice* are pronounced separately.

3   Additional examples might include: *departure time, lunch time, bookstore, rock music, folk music, right-handed; cab driver, bus driver, apple juice, grape juice, bath towel, color television.*

Either have students report their answers in class or collect them and use them to construct an exercise similar to **1** for further practice at a later time. Accept only answers in which the first word ends in a consonant sound.

If students report their answers in class, you could ask questions that call for a choice between the phrases here and the phrases in **1**. For example: *Which do you prefer, classical music or rock music?, Are you left-handed or right-handed?*

4   During repetition of the phrases in the boxes, monitor the link between the consonants at the word boundaries. In most cases, the consonant at the end of the first word should be released directly into the consonant at the beginning of the next word; for example, "li kethem," "that svery."

5   Follow the instructions in **4** for monitoring linking. Note that the following consonants would normally be dropped in connected speech: *and this.*

6   Follow the instructions in **4** for monitoring linking. Note that the following consonants would normally be dropped in connected speech: *last Friday, next March.*

Sequences in which the consonant that begins the second word is /ð/ or /θ/ are likely to be especially difficult for students. In a phrase like *missed them*, for example, the final /t/ in *missed* /mɪst/ is released into the /ð/ to form an affricate. Although students do not need to know the details of articulation here, they should be discouraged from adding an extra syllable for the *-ed* or from dropping the ending altogether. Rewriting this as "miss dthem" may help.

7   Follow the instructions in **4** for monitoring linking. Note that some native speakers drop the /d/ in *we'd better.*

8 **Answers**

    a. 6   two people talking about a rock group
    b. 4   two people talking about some pictures one of them has drawn or painted
    c. 7   two people talking about a missing car
    d. 5   two students talking about their homework

EXTENSION

To give students more practice with linking pairs of words with consonants, take a section from a conversation given in another book students are using in their classes. Ask students to first underline consonants they expect to hear across word boundaries. Either play the accompanying recording or make your own recording and play it. Students listen to the recording, noting how the consonants they have underlined are pronounced. They then repeat after the recording.

Unit 35 More on linking words together with consonants

This unit looks at some changes in pronunciation that take place when certain sequences of consonants occur across word boundaries in connected speech. Since it is a fairly long unit, you may want to divide it into two separate lessons.

1, 2 During repetition of the phrases and practice in pairs, monitor the lengthening of the consonant at the word boundaries. Check to make sure that students link the words without adding a vowel between them

BACKGROUND

When the same consonant occurs across a word boundary, the consonant is usually lengthened. It is not pronounced twice. When the consonant involved is a stop (/p/, /b/, /t/, /d/, /k/, or /g/), there is one long closure, with the first stop held and not released until the second stop is said.

Note that the affricates /tʃ/ and /dʒ/ are exceptions. When two /tʃ/ or /dʒ/ sounds occur across a word boundary, as in *which chapter* or *orange juice*, the sound is pronounced twice. These consonants are not practiced here.

Also, if the first word in a phrase is unstressed (as in *for Robert, should drive, some more*), the identical consonant is not always lengthened.

Answers

We lost the game   one-nothing   .

Is there   enough food   for the party?

The   same man   called again.

Make a   right turn   at the corner.

Let's sit   on the couch.

She was driving a   black car   .

Would you like   more rice   ?

A   bad dream   woke me up.

EXTENSION

Ask students to make more phrases like the ones in **1**, using the words from column 1. They should make new phrases by adding a word that starts with the sound at the end of the first word (for example, *bad dog, more rain*). This can be done individually, in pairs, or for homework. You could also ask them to write a sentence using each phrase. These sentences could then form the basis for an exercise like the one in the Student's Book.

BACKGROUND

The focus in **3** through **6** is on changes in the pronunciation of the sounds /t/, /d/, and /n/ (alveolars, made with the tip of the tongue touching the tooth ridge, or alveolar ridge) when they are followed by words that begin with the sounds /m/, /b/, and /p/ (bilabials, made by closing the two lips) or /g/ and /k/ (velars, made with the back of the tongue touching the soft palate). In connected speech, the sounds /t/, /d/, and /n/ are often produced at a place in the mouth closer to the place where the following bilabial or velar consonants are produced. For example, in the phrase *brown bag*, the /n/ sound at the end of *brown* may be said almost as /m/ as the tongue and lips move quickly into position to produce the /b/ sound at the beginning of *bag*. In *ran quickly*, the /n/ sound may resemble /ŋ/ as the tongue moves into position for the /k/ sound at the beginning of *quickly*, making the phrase sound much like *rang quickly*. When a cluster with /nd/ or /nt/ is involved, as in *found both* or *went back*, both sounds in the cluster may be affected. The process of changing the pronunciation of a sound to make it sound more like a neighboring sound is often referred to as *assimilation*.

This unit does not look at the details of these changes in pronunciation. Although it is perhaps not of great importance for students to make such changes in their own speech, it is useful for them to be aware that such changes take place to help them understand the connected speech of native speakers.

4   Encourage students to run the consonants together and pronounce the consonant sounds in their connected speech form. You may want to point out some of the changes that occur at the end of the first word in each phrase.

6   If there is time, ask some of the pairs to choose a sentence to read to the rest of the class.

BACKGROUND

In **7** through **9**, the focus is still on changes in the pronunciation of alveolar consonants. When any of the alveolar consonants – /t/, /d/, /s/, or /z/ – are followed by a word that begins with the palatal consonant /y/, the two sounds may be blended together and pronounced as follows:

/t/ + /y/→/ʧ/	Don't forget your passport.
/d/ + /y/→/ʤ/	You won't need your jacket.
/s/ + /y/→/ʃ/	You'll miss your train.
/z/ + /y/→/ʒ/	Don't lose your camera.

This form of blending, which is often referred to as *palatalization*, is more likely to occur when the sound /y/ begins an unstressed word (like *your* in the examples above) than when /y/ comes at the beginning of a stressed word (like *yogurt* in *I bought yogurt*). It occurs very commonly in questions beginning *Did you . . ., Could you . . ., Don't you . . ., What's your . . ., Where's your . . ., How's your . . .*, and so on; you may want to give students some examples for additional practice. In general, palatalization may be more common with the sounds /t/ and /d/ than with /s/ and /z/. Although palatalization is especially likely in faster speech, it is not restricted to highly informal or very fast speech; it is common in relaxed conversation between native speakers. As with the changes in pronunciation practiced in **3** through **6**, though it is not necessary for students to use these palatalized pronunciations in their own speech, it is very important for them to be aware of such changes, which can often make the natural speech of native speakers difficult for learners to understand. With palatalization, a sentence like *What's your name*, for example, can sound rather close to *Watch your name*.

8   After students listen and repeat, write *put your* on the board and ask students to say how the two linked sounds are pronounced. (They are pronounced as /ʧ/.) The palatalized pronunciation of the other words is shown in **7**.

9   Monitor the pronunciation of the linked consonants during pairwork. Encourage students to use the palatalized pronunciations. Though students may not need to incorporate this feature in their own speech, some productive practice is helpful for students to become more aware of and familiar with the feature.

EXTENSION

Record a conversation between native speakers that includes examples of palatalization. Have students either transcribe the whole conversation or fill in blanks in a partial transcription. Or give students a transcript of the conversation and have them mark places where palatalization occurs as they listen to a recording.

In very fast speech, palatalization may combine with other connected speech phenomena to produce such reduced forms as "Whereja go" /wɛrdʒəgow/ or "Whaja do" /wɑdʒəduw/ for *Where did you go?* and *What did you do?*; you may want to give advanced students practice with reductions like these.

UNIT 36   Sounds that link words: /w/ and /y/

BACKGROUND

When a word that ends in a vowel is followed by a word that begins with a vowel, speakers often insert a very short /w/ or /y/ sound to link the vowels together to make the flow of speech smoother and to avoid a gap between the words. The choice of /w/ or /y/ depends on the vowel at the end of the first word. If the vowel ends with the highest part of the tongue close to the *front* of the mouth (/iy/, /ey/, /ay/, /ɔy/), then the linking sound will be /y/. If the vowel is produced with the highest part of the tongue close to the *back* of the mouth (/uw/, /ow/, /aw/), then the linking sound will be /w/.

Note that other vowels are usually smoothly linked without adding a linking sound, although some speakers may add a glottal stop between them, as in *vanilla ice cream* or *law officer*.

1 Listening script

Joe: You know it's Brian's birthday on Thursday?
Mary Ann: Oh, I forgot all about it.
Joe: I suppose we should buy him a present.
Mary Ann: And we really ought to have a party or something for him.
Joe: Well, what can we get him? Do you have any ideas?
Mary Ann: It depends how much we want to spend.
Joe: If we pay about $20, we could get him something pretty nice.
Mary Ann: What about a new umbrella? He's got that old blue one, but it's all broken. He should just throw it away.
Joe: That's a good idea. And it won't be too expensive. And what about a party?
Mary Ann: Well, why don't we invite a few friends over here? How about Thursday evening?
Joe: Yeah, maybe . . . but I know he has an interview on Friday, and he might want to prepare for that.
Mary Ann: Well, let's wait till the weekend. Anyway, more people will be free on Saturday.
Joe: Yeah, let's do it Saturday. How about if I buy the present, and you arrange the party?
Mary Ann: OK.

Answers

1. On Thursday   2. An umbrella   3. On Saturday

5 In item 2, note that the *h* at the beginning of *him* would normally be silent here, so that the vowels in the two words *buy ̶him* are linked. "Disappearing" /h/ is dealt with in the next unit, Unit 37.

6 Answers

No, I didn't.
  w

Hi, Ann!
  y

There's no answer.
      w

Sunday afternoon.
     y

Can I try it?
     y

He must be at the office.
       y

Go ahead.
  w

Did you see it?
       y

When can you do it?
         w

Hi, how are you?
     w

Note that *the* before a vowel is usually pronounced /ðiy/, so that *the office* (in *He must be at the office*) would also have a linking /y/. Some speakers pronounce *the* as /ðə/, however, even before a vowel, especially in relaxed conversation. Only the link between *be* and *at* is marked here.

___

EXTENSION

Ask students to try to discover when /w/ is used to link words and when /y/ is used (for example, in the sentences in **6**). If necessary, give a clue by telling them to pay attention to the vowel sound that comes before the linking sound.

___

8 Answers

The following are the most likely conversations:

A: Did you see it?
B: No, I didn't.

A: Hi, Ann.
B: Hi, how are you?

A: There's no answer.
B: He must be at the office.

A: When can you do it?
B: Sunday afternoon.

A: Can I try it?
B: Go ahead.

UNIT 37 Short sounds and disappearing /h/

1 Unstressed /ə/ at the beginning of words is often very short and can be difficult for students to hear, especially in connected speech. If your students have particular difficulty with this, you could give additional practice with pairs of words that contrast the presence and absence of initial unstressed /ə/; for example, *along/long, away/way, across/cross, asleep/sleep, awake/wake, ago/go, around/round, estate/state, esteem/steam, alive/live, aside/side.*

3 Answers

1. A: Where does she live?
   B: Just __across__ the street.
2. A: Do you think I'm right?
   B: Yes, I __agree__ completely.
3. A: Can't you sleep?
   B: No, I've been __awake__ for hours.
4. A: When did you move here?
   B: Two years __ago__ .

5. A: Don't you get lonely in that big house?
   B: No, I like living __alone__ .
6. A: Is the bank near here?
   B: Yes, it's __about__ five minutes __away__ .
7. A: Can I speak to David?
   B: Sorry, he's __asleep__ right now.
8. A: Have you seen my keys?
   B: Yes, they're __around__ here somewhere.

Students should use the conversational contexts to help identify the missing words. You might point out that although pairs of words with and without initial unstressed /ə/ may sound similar in connected speech, they usually function differently in sentences – as with *across* (preposition or adverb) and *cross* (verb or noun) – which helps in identifying them. All the missing words here begin with unstressed /ə/.

BACKGROUND

When words begin with the sound /h/, this sound is often made very short or may be lost altogether in connected speech. This "disappearing /h/" (focused on in **3** through **6**) occurs especially in some very common words that have a strong and weak form (for more information on strong and weak forms, see the notes for Unit 28 and the units in Part 7). These words include *had, has, have, he, her, him, his,* and *who,* which are pronounced with an initial /h/ sound in their strong forms. The /h/ may be left out in their weak forms when these words occur in connected speech within a sentence. The /h/ is pronounced in the weak forms, however, if the word occurs at the beginning of a sentence or after a pause.

It is not necessary for students to incorporate this feature into their own speech for them to be understood, though it does facilitate linking. It is, however, important for students to be aware of disappearing /h/ to help them understand the connected speech of native speakers. This is why the emphasis in this unit is on understanding and identification, not production.

4 Answers

1. A: Have they found him?
   B: Who?
   A: The man who robbed your house.

2. A: Did h̸e tell h̸er what happened?
   B: He did, but she didn't believe h̸im.

3. A: How's Henry these days?
   B: Didn't you hear about h̸is heart attack?

4. A: Did you call h̸im?
   B: He wasn't home. He must h̸ave left already.

5. A: It says here that the President's coming.
   B: Where's h̸e going to be?
   A: Here.
   B: Oh, I hope we'll be able to see h̸im.

6. A: What are you children fighting about?
   B: It's MY book.
   C: HIS book's over THERE.
   B: HER book's over there. This one's mine!

5 Answers

who, he, her, his, have
The sound /h/ is pronounced when these words are at the beginning of a sentence or are given special emphasis.

Note that *him* also follows this rule, but does not occur in the conversations in **4** in the contexts in which /h/ is pronounced.

6 Point out to students that when /h/ is dropped, the preceding word is linked to the vowel that follows /h/. If necessary, mark these links for students. It can be helpful to rewrite some of the linked words without *h* and without a space between the words (for example, "foundim," "teller") or to use respellings that show the way the linked words should sound (for example, "diddy" for *did he*).

EXTENSION

If you have worked through all of the units in Part 5, it may be useful to give students the opportunity to see how all the features they have studied are found in connected speech. To do this, begin by reminding students of the features they have practiced. For example, write the summary below on a handout or on the board:

Here are common features of connected speech:

1. Links between consonants and vowels	Example: seven oranges
2. Links between different consonants	Example: six books
3. Links between the same consonants	Example: that time
4. Links between the consonants /t/, /d/, and /n/ and the consonants /m/, /b/, /p/, /g/, or /k/	Examples: that man, more expensive than gold

sity Press, 1986) and *Intonation and Its Uses* (Stanford University Press, 1989), D. Bradford, *Intonation in Context* (Cambridge University Press, 1988), and D. Brazil, *The Communicative Value of Intonation in English* (University of Birmingham, 1985).

UNIT 38 Prominent words

BACKGROUND

Prominent words stand out from the surrounding words. This may be because they are said with a longer vowel in the stressed syllable, said slightly louder than other words, said at a different (usually higher) pitch, or said with a falling or rising pitch. For example, if you listen to the recording of sentence 5 in Unit 38, **1**, in the Student's Book, you should hear the word *sure* as prominent in *I'm sure she will.*

Although we talk here about prominent and nonprominent *words*, if you listen to a sentence such as sentence 6 in Unit 38, **1**, *He's my uncle*, you will hear that it is only the first syllable of *uncle* that is prominent. However, it is a useful simplification to say that the word *uncle* is prominent, even though only one of its syllables is prominent. Any word that has a prominent syllable will be said to be prominent. In some of the tasks in Part 6, prominent words are shown in capital letters. The whole word is written in capital letters even though in words with more than one syllable, only one of the syllables is actually prominent.

It is important to distinguish here what we mean by *stress* and what we mean by *prominence*. When you look up a word with more than one syllable in a dictionary, one of these syllables is marked as having stress; for example, *com 'pu ter* or *com pu'ter*. Some words will have two stresses, one primary and the other secondary; for example, *ˌJap a 'nese*. When a word is used in connected speech, it may or may not be given prominence. If it is, then the prominent syllable in the word will be the one that the dictionary indicates is stressed.

For example, a dictionary will say that the word *raining* has stress on the first syllable, and that the word *again* has stress on the second. If you listen to sentence 8 in Unit 38, **1**, you will hear that *raining* is prominent, but *again* is not. So not all stressed syllables are prominent, but if a word *is* made prominent, then the stressed syllable becomes the prominent one. In words with both primary and secondary stress, the primary stressed syllable will normally be made prominent, although sometimes it may be the one having secondary stress in a word with moving stress (see Unit 30).

A word that is made prominent is typically chosen from a range of words that are possible in a context rather than being a word that fills a grammar function, such as a pronoun, preposition, or an article. So, for example, in sentence 7 in Unit 38, **1**, *He's an accountant*, the word *accountant* is made prominent, but not the word *he*. *Accountant* is a choice from a range of jobs (teacher, librarian, and so on), while, if the topic of conversation is a particular male person, then the speaker must use *he* here – there is no other choice. Many grammar words such as pronouns are normally nonprominent, because they are not usually a selection from a range of possible words. (They can, of course, be prominent if there is a choice or contrast involved, as in the sentence *I'm not going but he is.*)

1 Explain that one word in each sentence here is prominent. If appropriate for your students, discuss the features that make a word (more accurately, the stressed syllable in the word) prominent in English: a longer vowel, a change in pitch (usually, a higher pitch), and/or greater loudness.

You could ask students to read the sentences before listening to the recording and try to predict which word would be prominent in each. Then have them listen to the recording and decide if their predictions were correct.

Answers

1. (Thank) you.
2. I'm (tired).
3. (Chris) did.
4. It's getting (late).
5. I'm (sure) she will.

6. He's my (uncle).
7. He's an (accountant).
8. It's (raining) again.
9. She's in the (living) room.
10. She (told) me about it.

2 During repetition, make sure that the circled words are made clearly prominent, and that students do not rush through them. If necessary, remind students to slow down. Make sure, too, that students do not put emphasis on the words *not* marked as prominent.

3 Answers

a.	3	f.	6
b.	1	g.	2
c.	7	h.	4
d.	8	i.	9
e.	10	j.	5

4 Note that the words shown in capital letters in **3** are those made prominent on the recording. Since decisions about prominence are somewhat subjective, different speakers might make different choices, and the number of words given prominence in a particular sentence could vary. For example, in sentence e, only two of the three words marked (for example, just *Donna* and *house*) might be said as prominent.

5 When students practice the conversations, check to make sure that they make only one syllable in each circled or capitalized word prominent. Give them one or two examples to show that only one syllable in a word like *dinner* (in **3**, sentence a) or *accountant* (in **1**, sentence 7) should be prominent.

6 Answers

1. Content words – for example, nouns (like *time*), verbs (like *told*), and adjectives (like *tired*) – are typically   prominent   .
2. Grammar words – for example, pronouns (like *she*), articles (like *a*), and preposi-tions (like *about*) – are typically   not prominent   .

The use of prominence helps the listener know what is important or new in a sentence. Explain or elicit that since content words generally give more informa-tion than grammar words, they are more likely to be made prominent. Content words are generally chosen from a range of words that are possible in the context, while with grammar words, there is often no choice (see *Background*). The rules here can only serve as a rough guide, since any word can be made prominent if it is important in the context.

You could ask students to find examples of content words and grammar words in the sentences in **1** and **3**, in addition to those given in the rules, and to note whether these words were marked as prominent or not. Additional examples of content words from these tasks include *uncle, accountant, living (room), Chris, dinner* (nouns); *raining, thank, bought* (verbs); and *sure, late,* (adjectives). (Although adverbs are generally considered to be content words, they are sometimes prominent and sometimes not, depending on the type of adverb and its position in the sentence; for example, the adverb *quickly* in *I walked quickly* is likely to be prominent, but the adverb *again* in *It's raining again* is not.) Additional examples of grammar words in **1** and **3** include *I, he, it, me, you* (pronouns); *the* (article); *in, for* (prepositions); and *did, will,* and *is* (auxiliary verbs). Note that *wh-* question words (*who, what,* and so on) are often prominent. Note, too, that even when *is, are,* and other forms of *be* are main verbs (and not auxiliaries), they are typically not prominent. As with any grammar-based rules about prominence, exceptions can readily be found (for example, *Who IS it?*, with prominence on *is* and not on the *wh-* word, as said in response to a knock on the door).

7 Answers

The following are the most likely answers:

Indian specialties: chicken/shrimp/vegetable curry
Mexican specialties: chicken/cheese enchiladas
Chinese specialties: chicken/shrimp/vegetable lo mein
Japanese specialties: shrimp/vegetable tempura
American selections: apple/cherry pie

8 Listening script

chicken curry	vegetable curry
cheese enchiladas	chicken enchiladas
shrimp lo mein	shrimp tempura
vegetable tempura	cherry pie
apple pie	

Note that both words are made prominent here, a common pattern in modifier plus noun combinations (see Unit 25, **6**).

10 Monitor prominence when students work in groups. When a word is repeated in the conversations (either by the same speaker or another speaker), it should not be made prominent. Students can order from the menu in the book, or from real restaurant menus that you have brought to class.

Listening script

Waitress: Are you ready to order?
Customer 1: Yes, I think so.
Waitress: What will you have?
Customer 1: I think I'll have enchiladas. Chicken enchiladas.
Waitress: Chicken enchiladas. And for you, sir?
Customer 2: I'd like curry. Vegetable curry.
Waitress: Vegetable curry. OK. And how about dessert?
Customer 1: Mm. Let me see. Maybe some pie. Apple pie.
Waitress: Apple pie. And for you?
Customer 2: I'd like cherry pie.
Waitress: OK. One apple pie and one cherry pie. Thank you.

UNIT 39   Repeated words and prominence

BACKGROUND

Many learners of English tend to make more words prominent than they should. Units 39 and 40 give practice by focusing on words that are rarely prominent – repeated words and certain grammar words, particularly pronouns. Words that are prominent typically give new information or make a contrast. Words that are repeated in a conversation do not, by their very nature, give new information, and so they typically are not prominent. Grammar words are usually not prominent; they tend to carry little of the information load and are often predictable from the context or (as in the case of pronouns) simply repeat information.

1   Listening script

3. A: Do you have any in dark blue?
   B: NO, SORRY, only LIGHT blue.
4. A: Are you feeling better?
   B: Oh, YES. MUCH better.
5. A: Should we meet at one?
   B: Can we MAKE it a QUARTER AFTER one?
6. A: And the winning number is 5-4-9.
   B: That's MY number.
7. A: Is he an artist?
   B: ACTUALLY, a VERY GOOD artist.
8. A: Did you say Tom was in the front yard?
   B: NO, the BACKyard.

Notice that the repeated word is not made prominent. Monitor prominence when students say B's part, and check that the repeated word is not made prominent.

EXTENSION

Direct attention to words that *are* made prominent in B's part in **1**, perhaps asking students to underline them. Notice that some of these words contrast with words in A's part (for example, *dark blue/light blue, front yard/backyard*), while others offer new information (for example, *an artist/a very good artist*).

---

2 In this activity, monitoring is to be done by one of the students in each group. If organizing students into groups of three is difficult, this could be done in pairs with the teacher monitoring.

3 Listening script

In the middle of the picture is a big circle, and just above it is a small circle. To the left of the big circle is a small triangle, and to the right is a big triangle.

Answer

b

4 Answers

In the middle is a big circle.
Above it is a small circle.

To the left of the big circle is a small triangle.
To the right is a big triangle.

Point out or elicit that the repeated words are not made prominent.

5 Demonstrate this first with a student. Draw a picture on a piece of paper and describe it to the student, who should try to draw the picture on the board. Then compare your picture with what the student drew and point out any differences. During pairwork, monitor prominence particularly on *big, small, circle, square,* and *triangle*. Draw attention to repeated words that should not be made prominent.

EXTENSION

If possible, record one or two pairs of students doing the activity in **5** and note any difficulties with prominence. Replay the recording to the class and point out the problems. Ask what *should* have been said.

Part 6 / Intonation　　**101**

UNIT 40 More on prominent and nonprominent words

1 Answers

1. them
2. her
3. there
4. he

5. him
6. there
7. one
8. us

2 The point of the activity in **1**–and the explanation that should be elicited or given in **2**–is that it is not only repeated items that are often nonprominent, but also *pronouns* (and adverbs like *there*). These can be seen as a way of repeating the noun (or phrase) to which they refer and do not give any new information.

BACKGROUND

Time expressions are the focus of **4** through **9**. Some expressions of time are normally prominent; for example, expressions of time that include numbers or certain words such as *every: We're moving on June first; I have an appointment at 2:30; I eat lunch there every day*. But some expressions of time are often seen as "background," or unimportant information, and are typically *not* prominent at the end of a sentence. These include words and phrases like *today, tomorrow, yesterday, this morning, last night, this year, next week, soon, now, yet,* and *lately,* in sentences such as the following: *Where did you have lunch today?; We're going away next weekend; She said she would call soon.*

However, any of these time expressions can be made prominent if the information is felt to be important. Three situations in which this is likely are when the expression of time: (1) answers a question about time (e.g., A: *When did you see Anna?* B: *I just saw her this morning*); (2) focuses or puts emphasis on when something happened or will happen (e.g., A: *I hear you found a new apartment.* B: *Yes, I'm moving tomorrow*); or (3) contrasts with another expression of time (e.g., A: *Do you want to go to the beach today?* B: *Not really. I went to the beach yesterday*). More information about this approach to prominent and nonprominent time expressions can be found in W. Dickerson, *Stress in the Speech Stream* (University of Illinois Press, 1989).

5 Answers

1. –
2. ✓
3. ✓
4. –

5. –
6. ✓,✓
7. ✓
8. ✓

This exercise may be challenging for students, but time expressions are very common in conversation, and many students tend to make too many of them prominent. It is important to practice time expressions in a conversational context, because it is often the context that determines whether or not they will be prominent.

Notice that in time expressions consisting of more than one word, sometimes only one word is prominent. For example, in sentence 3, only *last* in *last night* would be prominent, since this is the part that specifically contrasts with *tonight* in A's question.

7, 9 You may want to point out that in the examples in **7** and the phrases in **9**, the two people are talking about the same subject even though the words they use to describe it may be different. So, for example, *out to eat* is the same as *to a restaurant* (and is not prominent in the man's response).

Notice that in the responses, there is prominence on the time expression even if it is one that is typically not prominent (for example, *last night* or *this morning*). The speaker is making a contrast between the time frame of the suggestion and the previous time that the activity was done.

Answers

The following are the most likely answers:

1. LET'S visit your SISTER.   I SAW Lynn on WEDNESDAY.
2. LET'S go to the THEATER.   I SAW a play on TUESDAY.
3. LET'S go for a WALK.   I WENT to the park this MORNING. (or: I WENT to the PARK this MORNING.)
4. LET'S watch TV.   I WATCHED TV this AFTERNOON.

Monitor prominence during pairwork.

UNIT 41 Falling and rising intonation

BACKGROUND

This unit introduces the two most basic intonation patterns of English: falling intonation and rising intonation. These two intonations are practiced here only at the ends of sentences, where the difference between falling and rising intonation is easiest to hear and probably most crucial.

In North American English, a falling intonation generally first jumps up on the most prominent syllable (i.e., the syllable that is made to stand out by this rise) and then abruptly falls; it is sometimes referred to as rising-falling intonation. The fall can occur either immediately after the most prominent syllable, as in PARty in *I met him at a party*, or during this syllable, as in yourSELF in *Help yourself*, where nothing follows. (These examples are taken from Unit 41, **1**.)

Rising intonation jumps up on or just after the most prominent syllable and stays up or continues to rise even higher.

Falling intonation is associated with certainty and with giving new information. A fall to a low note, the intonation pattern practiced here, suggests completeness. Rising intonation is associated with incompleteness or uncertainty. It may also suggest that what is said is seen as old information, something already known.

1 Explain that Units 41 through 43 practice the melody, or tune, of English sentences – the pattern of high and low notes as the voice rises and falls. To demonstrate the melody of a sentence, it can be helpful to hum it (perhaps using a kazoo). Although students are asked only to listen to the examples, you may want to have them first try humming the sentences and then say the words in the sentences while keeping the melody.

Notice that both questions and statements are included here as examples for both types of intonation. Students should be discouraged from assuming, for example, that questions always rise at the end and statements fall. If necessary, explain that *Maybe* said with rising intonation would probably mean something like "maybe – maybe not."

2 Answers

1. THANKS ↘
2. My KEY ↗
3. CREAM ↗
4. There's some CAKE left ↘
5. EIGHTY DOLLARS ↘
6. I'm HUNGRY ↘
7. Can't you GUESS ↗
8. On the TABLE ↘
9. HOW much IS it ↘
10. I DRINK it BLACK ↘
11. Are you going to BUY it ↗
12. In the KITCHEN ↗
13. WHAT ↘
14. I FOUND something ↘
15. COFFEE ↗
16. It's TOO EXPENSIVE ↘

Punctuation is omitted in order to force students to rely on intonation alone to get the answers. Notice that the meaning of a sentence can change depending on which intonation pattern is used. For example, item 13 *(What)* said with rising intonation would ask for repetition, but said with falling intonation asks for new information. (There is more practice of this distinction in the next unit.) *In the kitchen* (item 12) said with falling intonation would probably be a statement giving information about location; said with rising intonation, it would probably be a question about location.

Note that students sometimes confuse the initial rise that occurs in falling intonation with rising intonation.

3 Rising and falling hand gestures can be used to signal corrections, if necessary, when students repeat the sentences.

EXTENSION

1. Have students add the missing punctuation to the sentences in **2**.
2. If students have difficulty hearing or producing a distinction between falling and rising intonation, you could give additional practice in discriminating between the two. For example, say a sentence (this could consist of a single word) using either rising or falling intonation; students say which intonation they heard. If you write the sentences on the board or a handout, students could practice this in pairs or in groups of three (with one person saying the sentences, one identifying which intonation was used, and one monitoring the intonation). Here are some examples of possible sentences to use: *OK; That's all; Nobody told him; Turn left here; Do you think so; What did you say; Yes; Lucy.*

4 Answers

1. A: 6	2. A: 11	3. A: 14	4. A: 15
B: 4	B: 16	B: 13	B: 1
A: 12	A: 9	A: 7	A: 3
B: 8	B: 5	B: 2	B: 10

Students have to arrange the sentences in **2** to form coherent conversations. Consideration of the intonation pattern is crucial for doing this. Encourage students to say the sentences aloud as they try to form the conversations.

5 If it seems helpful for your students, have them repeat each conversation one line at a time before practicing in pairs.

You may want to have students work in groups of three rather than in pairs, with one student monitoring the intonation of the others.

Focus on falling intonation

6 Point out that *red* and *blue* give new information, so they are said with falling intonation. And both questions beginning with *what* here ask for new information. You might also want to call attention to words that are prominent or nonprominent. Note that *favorite* is not prominent when it is repeated. *My* in the last sentence is made prominent because it contrasts with *your*.

7 During pairwork, monitor intonation. If students have difficulty, you could ask them to hum the lines of the conversation.

Students could be asked to report back the information they found out.

8 You may want to break this activity up between two class periods so that you can correct any errors in the questions and answers. Students will need to circulate around the room for the second part of the activity, saying their question or answer until they find the person who has the matching answer or question. Encourage students to memorize their question or answer before saying it to other students. You may want to set a time limit (say, five or ten minutes, depending on class size). At the end, ask the matched pairs of students to say their questions and answers. You could also ask students to identify the part of the answer that is (or should be) prominent, which is the part that specifically answers the question.

Note that it is not obligatory to use falling intonation in the questions. Questions like these that ask about matters of general knowledge are sometimes said with rising intonation at the end, to suggest that the information is old – for example, something previously known to, but now forgotten by, the speaker. If students use rising intonation in their questions, you may want to discuss this distinction – that falling intonation suggests they are asking for new information, while rising intonation might suggest they are asking about something previously known or discussed.

Focus on rising intonation

BACKGROUND

One common use of rising intonation is in *yes-no* questions. This does not mean, however, that *yes-no* questions always, or even usually, have rising intonation. Studies have shown that falling intonation is also quite common in *yes-no* questions (see, for example, C. C. Fries, "On the Intonation of 'Yes/No' Questions in English" in D. Abercrombie, D. B. Fry, P. A. D. McCarthy, N. C. Scott, and J. L. M. Trim, *In Honor of Daniel Jones* [Longman, 1964]).

And although it is not practiced here, rising intonation is also used at the end of statements, especially by younger people who use what is sometimes referred to as *uptalk* or *upspeak*. Here is a real example from a young waiter in a restaurant:

We have a special tonight. It's salmon.

10 Answers

A: Are you tired?
B: Do I look tired?

A: Are you ready?
B: Is it time to leave already?

A: Should I close the window?
B: Are you cold?

A: Have you seen my keys?
B: Did you lose them again?

A: Could I borrow a dollar?
B: Do you need it now?

A: Wasn't that a great movie?
B: Did you really like it?

Point out that you can often answer a question with another question.

EXTENSION

Give students some additional *yes-no* questions. Ask them to work in pairs and for each question, think of another question that could be used as a response.

UNIT 42
More on falling and rising intonation

Asking someone to repeat

BACKGROUND

As seen in Unit 41, falling intonation is often used in questions that ask for new information. Rising intonation, which is associated with uncertainty and with old information, is often used when asking someone to repeat. Compare, for example, *What?* said with falling intonation, which asks for new information, and *What?* said with rising intonation, which asks for repetition (that is, old information).

Rising intonation can be used in various ways to ask for repetition. Some general ways to ask someone to repeat with rising intonation are shown in Unit 42, **1**, and *wh-* questions that check specific information by use of rising intonation are practiced in Unit 42, **2** through **5**. It is also possible to use a *wh-* word alone with rising intonation to ask for repetition, for example:

A: *I'm going to China in the fall.*

B: *When?*

Or the first speaker's words can be repeated with rising intonation to ask for confirmation, for example:

A: *I'm going to China in the fall.*

B: *In the fall?*

Asking someone to repeat something not clearly heard or understood – and especially asking someone to confirm specific information – is, of course, a useful skill for ESL students to have.

1 Notice that the use of rising intonation to ask for repetition can occur with any of various types of grammatical structures, as in the example sentences here and the examples in Unit 41. Also note that the sentences shown here can be used with other intonation patterns, but would then have functions other than asking for repetition.

2 Point out that the examples in **1** give some common but not very precise ways of asking someone to repeat. By using *wh-* questions, as in the conversation on the left in **2**, speakers can focus on the piece of information they want to check.

Notice the difference in the words given prominence in the questions in the two conversations. In the question asking for new information, both the *wh-* question word and *going* are prominent, with the fall in intonation occurring on *going* (the focus word; see Unit 44). In the question asking for repetition, only the question word is made prominent, with the rise in intonation starting on that word (the focus word).

3 When students repeat, make sure the rise in the question asking for repetition is not too sharp. A very high or sharp rise may suggest surprise or disbelief rather than a simple request to repeat.

4 Listening script

The arrows indicate the intonation of B's questions.

1. A: I'm going to California next week.
   B: Where?

2. A: We're moving to New York next month.
   B: When are you moving?

3. A: I bought that rug in Mexico.
   B: Where?

4. A: I tried to call you last night.
   B: When?

5. A: Richard left a present for you.
   B: What?

6. A: My mother works in an office.
   B: What does she do?

7. A: I have an appointment on Tuesday.
   B: When is your appointment?

8. A: Someone I work with gave me this cassette.
   B: Who?

Answers

1. California.
2. On the fifteenth.
3. In Mérida, at an outdoor market.
4. Around nine o'clock.
5. I said, Richard left a present for you.
6. She's a receptionist.
7. On Tuesday.
8. Linda Novak.

5 Demonstrate the task with a couple of students. If it is difficult to arrange your class into groups of three, students could work in pairs, with the teacher monitoring when possible.

Giving choices

BACKGROUND

The intonation for giving choices is typically to have rising intonation on each choice until the last. For example:

Would you like the red one, the blue one, or the green one?

Questions like these are often called alternative questions. The last item has falling intonation, showing that the speaker has finished. As with other structures, other intonation patterns may also be possible.

Note that questions with *or* do not always ask the listener to make a choice. Sometimes they ask for a *yes* or *no* answer. The intonation for this kind of question is usually like that of any other *yes-no* question, with one intonation (often rising at the end) for the whole sentence. Compare these two questions. For example:

Do you want a large or small box? (alternative question)

Does the price include tax or service? (*yes-no* question)

Often *yes-no* questions with *or* can be answered either with one of the choices or with *yes* or *no*. For example:

A: *Does the price include tax or service?*
B: *Just tax. / No.*

7 Prominence, practiced in Units 38 to 40, is recycled here in a new context. Notice that in alternative questions, each of the choices mentioned is made prominent. With your students, read through the notes given about words in the conversation, explaining further if necessary.

Monitor both prominence and intonation (rising on the first choice, falling on the second) when students repeat the conversation.

8 You may want to demonstrate the task with a student, showing that students should follow the same pattern as in the example conversation, substituting words from the box or other words they can think of. Here is an example:

A: Can you get some bananas?
B: Do you want a large or small bunch?
A: A large one.

EXTENSION

Explain that questions with *or* do not always ask you to make a choice. Sometimes they ask for a *yes* or *no* answer. The intonation patterns are different. For example:

Is the Grand Canyon in New Mexico or Arizona? (choice)

Would you like something to eat or drink? (*yes* or *no* answer).

Prepare a handout with questions such as those below. Ask the questions, using either choice or *yes-no* intonation. Students should respond with an appropriate answer based on the intonation you used. Then have students practice this in pairs (or groups of three, with a third student monitoring) Note that it is often possible to answer the *yes-no* type question with one of the choices:

A: *Do you speak French or Spanish?*

B: *Just Spanish.*

However, it is not possible to answer a choice question simply with *yes* or *no*.

1. Do you speak French or Spanish?
   Spanish.
   No, I don't.
2. Do you play soccer or softball?
   Softball.
   Yes, both.
3. Do you want to go for a walk or drive?
   Let's go for a walk.
   Not right now.
4. Would you like blue cheese or Italian dressing?
   Blue cheese.
   No, thanks.
5. Would you like to read a newspaper or magazine while you wait?
   A magazine, please.
   No, thanks. I brought a book.
6. Do you have office hours on Monday or Tuesday?
   On Monday.
   No, just on Wednesday.
7. Water or juice?
   Juice, please.
   No, thanks.
8. Does it have a washing machine or dryer?
   A washing machine.
   Yes.

BACKGROUND

This unit focuses on two major functions of intonation – dividing sentences into thought groups and signaling that what is said is either complete or incomplete. The unit also introduces a third type of intonation – falling-rising intonation. Falling-rising intonation begins by jumping up and falling, but that it does not fall to as low a pitch as the falling intonation practiced in the preceding units. It then rises very slightly. What is most important for learners – more important than the final rise – is to make sure the voice does not drop too low, which would suggest a sentence-final, "complete" intonation.

Note that there is another type of falling-rising intonation that is not practiced here. In this type of intonation, the voice starts high and jumps *down* in pitch on the most prominent syllable (rather than jumping up to the most prominent syllable), and then rises a little. This intonation is often used, for example, in polite requests for information (e.g., *How do I get to Wall Street?*). It might also be heard in a sentence like *He won't hurt you.*

1 Explain that in longer sentences, speakers group words together into *thought groups*. Each thought group ends with a change in intonation and often a pause, though the pause may not be very noticeable. Point out that the sentences here all end with falling intonation, where the intonation jumps up on the last prominent syllable and then falls to a low note. Since this intonation shows that the speaker is finished, it is used only at the end of a sentence. Other types of intonation are used for thought groups earlier in the sentence: rising intonation, falling-rising intonation, or falling intonation that falls only slightly and does not fall to a low note (only the first two are practiced here). Note that some learners have a tendency to drop their voices too low at the end of a nonfinal thought group.

You may want to mark the thought groups in the example sentences, showing a slash (/) at the end of each, with a double slash at the end of the sentence: *Turn left here/ and then go straight.// After we eat/ we could go and see Alison.// If I have to work late,/ I'll call you.//* The intonations given in the Student's Book are those used on the recording, but other nonfinal intonations are possible.

Although students are asked only to listen here, they may find it helpful to try repeating the sentences. Some people find it easier to feel what their own voice is doing than to hear distinctions that another speaker makes.

EXTENSION

To practice saying the example sentences in **1**, students could be asked to work in pairs and write short (two-line) conversations in which each of the example sentences occurs as the second line. For example: A: *How do I get to the bus station?* B: *Turn left here and then go straight.* It is often a good idea to practice intonation within a discourse context rather than in isolated sentences.

---

2 Answers

1. B	6. A
2. A	7. B
3. A	8. B
4. B	9. A
5. B	10. A

Explain the task. Tell students that if what they hear sounds as if it is missing something at the end – that is, if it sounds like the first part of a sentence – they should write A. If it sounds like the end of a sentence, they should write B. Point out that the B parts fall to a low note at the end. The A parts end with rising intonation – either a simple rise or a slight rise that occurs after a fall.

3 Answers

You can lead a horse to water, but you can't make him drink.
Don't count your chickens before they're hatched.
If you can't stand the heat, get out of the kitchen.
When in Rome, do as the Romans do.
It isn't whether you win or lose – it's how you play the game.

When students report their answers, it is probably best to accept any of the nonfinal types of intonation in the first parts of the sentences – rising, falling-rising, or falling slightly. The important point is that the voice should not drop to a low note before the end of the sentence.

EXTENSION

Collect the sayings from their native languages that students have written down in **3** and use these to construct an exercise similar to that in **2** and **3**. This will work best, of course, if students come from different language backgrounds, so that the halves of sayings will not be immediately recognizable to all the students.

---

5 Answers

1. C	6. O
2. O	7. C
3. O	8. C
4. C	9. C
5. O	10. O

BACKGROUND

The same kinds of intonation that are used in the first part of a sentence to show that the speaker is not finished can also be used at the end of a sentence, to show that something more could be said. A rise at the end leaves things "up in the air," with the sentence open to continuation or further comment. The open sentences here – the sentences that sound incomplete in some way – include both sentences with unfinished lists of items and sentences in which something is left unsaid. What is left unsaid might be a reservation, an unexpressed "but . . ." that could complete the sentence, or something that logically follows from what was said. (See, for example, the possible endings shown for sentences 1 and 7 in **5**, given in Unit 43, **6**.) A final rise can also suggest that the speaker is unsure about what he or she is saying. (For more on rising intonation, see *Background* to Unit 41, under Focus on rising intonation.)

Note that the unfinished lists end with rising intonation, and the sentences with something left unsaid end with falling-rising intonation, though it is not necessary for students to discriminate between these two types of intonation here. It is only necessary for them to distinguish between these two and the closed sentences, which end with a fall to a low note.

6 Students need to imagine here that all the sentences in **5** are said as open sentences that are incomplete in some way and to think of ways to complete them. You may want to ask students for another example or two to make sure they have understood the task.

Answers

The following are some possible answers:

1. We need bread and milk and bananas and onions.
2. He draws well, but he doesn't know how to paint.
   He draws well, and he probably paints well, too.
3. I like her sister, but I don't like her.
   I like her sister, so I'll probably like the rest of her family.
4. The restaurant isn't on Eighth Street; it's on Tenth Street.
5. We went to Spain and Portugal and France and Morocco.
6. It's possible, but it doesn't seem likely.
7. I'd like to see it, but I don't have time.
8. I thought you would, and you did.
   I thought you would, but you didn't.
9. I told you so, but you didn't believe me.
10. He seems nice, but he isn't.
    He seems nice, but I don't know him very well.

EXTENSION

Ask students to work in pairs. One partner should say each of the sentences in **5** with either open or closed intonation. The other partner should say which intonation was used.

7, 8 Answers

1. S B: YES ↘ – I'd LOVE to. ↘
2. D B: YES ↘ – I THINK so. ↗
3. S B: NO ↘↗ – not REALLY. ↘↗
4. D B: MAYBE ↘↗ – I don't KNOW yet. ↘
5. D B: REALLY ↗ – I THOUGHT they would. ↘
6. D B: On SUNDAY ↘ – if the WEATHER'S good. ↘↗

Students are first asked to decide only if the intonations used by B are different or the same. They are then asked to identify the three different intonation patterns they have learned; this is the first time they have been asked to differentiate all three types.

If students have difficulty (and some students may find the task here very difficult), it might help to ask questions that direct attention to the meaning entailed in B's choice of intonation. For example, does speaker B in the first conversation (*I'd love to*) sound as if she really wants to go for a drive? Or does she have reservations? Does the speaker in the second conversation (*I think so*) sound sure of himself or does he sound uncertain?

9 Monitoring in this task is to be done by the student's partner. Help or adjudicate where necessary. Encourage students to focus on the meaning the sentences have with the intonation used.

UNIT 44

Focus words

BACKGROUND

The word on which a fall or rise in intonation begins is here called the *focus word*. The choice of focus word is very important. Compare, for example, *It's on top of the bookcase*, which might be said in answer to *Where's the newspaper?*, and *It's on top of the bookcase*, which might be said in response to *I thought I put the newspaper in the bookcase*.

All focus words are heard as prominent, but not all prominent words are necessarily focus words. In Unit 44, **2**, sentence e, for example, both *five* and *after* are prominent, but only on *after* is there pitch movement. That is, only *after* is a focus word.

Focus words are very widely used in spoken English to highlight information that the speaker feels is important. They are typically used: (1) to signal information that is new (for example, A: *Do you play the piano?* B: *I used to play*); (2) to correct something said previously (for example, A: *Is this 549-6098?* B: *No, this is 549-6078*); or (3) to show a contrast with something else (for example, *Press the red one, not the black one*). Note that other languages often use other devices, such as word order or particles, to signal the focus of information. Students who are not aware of the way focus words are used in English may miss important cues when listening, as well as failing to use these cues themselves to highlight information when speaking.

1 Call attention to the focus words in the examples, pointing out that although other words in the sentence may also be prominent, only the word on which there is a pitch change is a focus word. To demonstrate the melody of the sentence, and the way the pitch changes on the focus word, it can be helpful to hum each sentence. Encourage students to hum the sentences, too.

You could give additional examples, showing the way focus words are used in even the most basic exchanges; for example: A: *What do you do?* B: *I work in a bank. What do you do?* Call attention to the way the focus shifts from *do* in A's question to *you* when B asks the same question.

2 Answers

a. It's on (top) of the bookcase.

b. With (milk,) please.

c. At (five) after one.

d. I (finished) it.

e. At five (after) one.

f. (I) finished it.

g. It's on top of the (bookcase.)

h. (With) milk, please.

4 Answers

1. h   5. d
2. c   6. a
3. g   7. e
4. b   8. f

Students have to match the sentences in **2** with the contexts created by the sentences in **4**. Consideration of placement of the focus word is crucial in doing this correctly.

EXTENSION

For more practice of focus words, write a sentence on the board; for example: *I like rock music.* Then ask questions or make statements that could have the sentence on the board as a response, but with varying choice of focus word. Here is an example (the focus word is underlined in the response in parentheses): *What kind of music do you like? (I like rock music.) Who likes rock music? (I like rock music.) Why are you listening to rock music? (I like rock music.) I thought you liked rock climbing. (I like rock music.) I thought you liked classical music. (I like rock music.)* You ask the questions or make the statements; students respond to each with the original sentence written on the board, choosing the appropriate focus word in each case. Other students should monitor the focus words, making sure that the correct one is chosen and that they can hear which one it is.

As an alternative, you could simply say one of the sentences in **4**; students respond with one of the sentences in **2**, choosing the appropriate word as focus word.

---

6 Answers

1. A: Can I help you?
   B: I'm looking for a coat.
   A: They're on the second floor.
   B: Thank you.

2. A: What do you think?
   B: I don't like the color.
   A: I thought you liked red.
   B: I prefer blue.

3. A: Should we eat here?
   B: Let's sit over there.
   A: Under that tree?
   B: The other one.

4. A: Can I speak to Rick?
   B: There's no Rick here.
   A: Is this 549-6098?
   B: No, this is 549-6078

With more advanced students, you may want to discuss the reasons for choosing particular focus words. You could also point out, or elicit, that the focus word in the first line of each conversation is the last content word in the sentence. This can, perhaps, be considered as the most neutral, or "default," placement of the focus word, since the important information in a sentence – especially at the beginning of a conversation – typically comes at the end in English.

EXTENSION

Many textbooks and supplementary materials include recordings of short two- or four-line conversations like these. Identify the focus words yourself in such conversations and then use them to construct an activity similar to the one in **6** through **8**.

---

9 One use of focus words is to correct something that has been said. In cases like this, the speaker will often put extra emphasis on the new, correct information.

UNIT 45

Predicting intonation

1 Answers

The following are the most likely answers:

1. A: It was EXPENSIVE.
   B: How MUCH?
   A: Two thousand DOLLARS.
   B: HOW much?

2. A: What's on TV tonight?
   B: A HORROR film.
   A: Is it GOOD?
   B: I've HEARD it is.

3. A: Where's LUCY?
   B: She went HOME.
   A: She LEFT?
   B: About an HOUR ago.

4. A: Is it still RAINING?
   B: I THINK so.
   A: HARD?
   B: Not VERY hard.

2 More advanced students could be asked the reasons for choosing the intonations they showed.

3 Monitor intonation during repetition and pairwork. If the intonation students use differs from the intonation marked in the answers shown above, try to get them to see what the different choices might mean. Often more than one intonation is possible.

5 Many contexts are possible for each of the sentences in **4**. Notice that the falling intonation in sentence 5 is likely to indicate a definite acceptance, perhaps of an invitation. The falling-rising intonation in sentence 6 is likely to indicate some sort of reservation: "I'd like to . . . but (I'm doing something else)." During performance, check that (1) the sentences are being said with the intonation shown and (2) the intonation is appropriate in the context that has been created.

EXTENSION

Although it is difficult to say that a particular emotion is signaled by a particular intonation, it can be fun for students to try using intonation to express different feelings. You can give students sentences and, for each, a few different situations in which the sentence might be said. Here is an example:

> Do you know what time it is?

Situations:

1. Someone asking a stranger on the street
2. A parent asking a teenager who has just returned home at 2:00 A.M.
3. Someone asking a neighbor who is playing loud music at 2:00 A.M.
4. Someone asking their husband/wife when both of them have overslept and missed their train

A student chooses, or is assigned, one of the situations and tries saying the sentence with an intonation that fits the situation. Other students then guess which situation was intended.

INTRODUCTION

Aims and organization

In Part 7, attention is drawn to the relationship between grammar and pronunciation in certain common and often problematic areas. These are (1) the weak and strong forms of auxiliary verbs, pronouns, conjunctions, and prepositions (weak forms often contain the unstressed vowel /ə/); (2) the long and short (or contracted) forms of auxiliary verbs; (3) the varying pronunciations of -*ed* endings in regular past tense verbs; and (4) the varying pronunciations of -*s* endings in noun plurals and third person singular present tense verbs.

Unit 46	Weak and strong forms (of *you* and the verbs *do, does,* and *can*); short and long forms (of the negatives of these verbs)
Unit 47	Long and short forms of verbs (*am, are, is, has, have, had, would, did,* and *will*)
Unit 48	Weak forms of some pronouns; more on the long and short forms of verbs
Unit 49	Weak forms of some conjunctions (*and, or, but, as,* and *than*)
Unit 50	Weak and strong forms of some prepositions (*at, for, from, of,* and *to*)
Unit 51	Pronouncing -*ed* endings (the pronunciation of the -*ed* ending of past tense verbs)
Unit 52	Pronouncing -*s* endings (the pronunciation of -*s* endings, with focus on noun plurals and third-person singular present tense verbs)

General notes

Students are sometimes resistant to using weak forms (for example, the pronunciation of *can* as /kən/) and short forms (contractions) because they think of them as features of "sloppy" or "lazy" speech. They may also be reluctant to use them because they feel that their speech will be clearer and more easily understood if they use full, unreduced forms. They may be especially resistant to using weak forms, which unlike short forms, are not indicated in writing. Failure to use weak and short forms, however, tends to interfere with English rhythm; native speakers do not give each word the same amount of stress. And probably more important, lack of familiarity with these forms interferes with listening comprehension.

Although students should be encouraged to use weak forms and short forms, they should not be forced to do so and, indeed, if their speech is otherwise slow and halting, weak forms may not sound natural. But it is essential for students to understand these forms when they hear them in order to understand the ordinary speech of native speakers. Practice in saying the forms will help students become familiar with them and be better able to understand them.

UNIT 46 Weak and strong forms; short and long forms

Weak and strong forms of you and the verbs do, does, and can

For background information on weak and strong forms, see *Background*, Unit 28.

1 The words pronounced with their weak forms are shown in smaller-sized letters. Note that strong forms can be said by themselves, but that weak forms occur only in a context.

Tell students that weak forms are very common in connected speech. The strong forms of the words are generally used in only a few situations: when the word is at the end of a phrase or sentence (i.e., before a pause, as in *Yes, I do, but not very often*) or when the word is given special emphasis (*But I do like you; He can't go but I can*). Otherwise, native speakers normally use weak forms, and strong forms may sound overly emphatic.

2, 3 During repetition, make sure that students use the weak forms of *does, you, do*, and *can*, shown in smaller type, pronouncing these words quickly with the unstressed vowel /ə/. In offering any correction needed, be careful not to emphasize the words or the sound /ə/. To avoid emphasis, it is best to say the words in a sentence or phrase rather than by themselves.

Note that although all the weak forms practiced in this unit contain unstressed /ə/, not all weak forms contain this vowel. The word *in*, for example, has the weak pronunciation /ɪn/, and the word *and* can be pronounced as a syllabic consonant /n/ (as in *hot and cold*), without any vowel.

4 Answers

No, next door. 3	In a zoo. 8	Yes, of course. 4
A little later. 2	Much better. 9	Tomorrow. 6
She's tired. 7	Not really. 5	Yes, very much. 1

Following are the short conversations:

1. Do you like it?   Yes, very much.
2. Can we go now?   A little later.
3. Does he live here?   No, next door.
4. Can I take two?   Yes, of course.
5. Does it hurt?   Not really.
6. When do you go back?   Tomorrow.
7. Why does she want to leave?   She's tired.
8. Where can we see one?   In a zoo.
9. How do you feel now?   Much better.

Short and long forms of negative verbs

BACKGROUND

While the term *weak form* refers to the pronunciation that certain individual words have when unstressed in connected speech, the term *short form* refers to a shortened combination in which two (or more) words are blended together. Short forms, often referred to as *contractions* or *contracted forms*, are very common in speech. They are less common in writing, but are used especially in writing in an informal or personal style. Note that most short forms are verbs, although *us* can also be contracted to *'s* in *let's*, as in *Let's go*).

In pronouncing the negative verbs here, notice that the *t* at the end of the short forms is often not clearly pronounced. It may be accompanied or replaced by a glottal stop, or dropped altogether before another word (for example, *In /dʌn/ ask*). For details on the pronunciation of /nt/ at the end of a word, see *Background* in Unit 20, **4**.

5 Point out that short forms are extremely common in speech and that the long forms of these negative verbs tend to sound very formal or emphatic in ordinary conversation. You may want to give some examples using these short forms: *I don't think so; It doesn't matter;* A: *Why don't you come with us?* B: *I can't. I have to work.*

You may also want to point out that the apostrophe in the written form goes where the letters from the long form are missing (for example, *do not→don't*).

6 It may be useful to demonstrate this activity first. Write the questions on the board and ask a student the questions. He or she should answer with the short forms, and you should write *Yes* or *No* as appropriate. If necessary, remind students to use short forms in negative answers and strong forms (because the verb is at the end of the sentence) in positive answers.

7 Demonstrate by reporting back the negative answers you gathered in **6**, as shown for the example in **7** in the Student's Book.

Can and can't

8 Many students have difficulty with the distinction between *can* and *can't* both in listening and speaking. Because the *t* in *can't* may be hard to hear (see **Background** under "Short and long forms of negative verbs" in this unit), often the main difference in sound between *can* and *can't* in connected speech is that *can* has the unstressed vowel /ə/ and *can't* has the full vowel /æ/.

Listening script

1. When can I see you?
2. She said she can come.
3. I can't find my glasses.
4. He can drive you to the airport.
5. I can't understand that.
6. You can't park here.
7. Can't he fix it?
8. We can walk there.

9 Explain the task. One student should make a statement about whether he or she can or can't do one of the activities in the box (or another activity). The other student should respond with a statement about himself/herself. If the information is the same, the second student should say "So can I" or "Neither can I," as appropriate. If the information is different, the second student should say "Oh, I can" or "Oh, I can't." Model this with a few students. You could tell students that the statements they make do not have to be true.

If it seems more appropriate for your class, have students work in groups of three, with one student monitoring the pronunciation of *can/can't* used by the other two students. Students should take turns being monitor.

UNIT 47 Long and short forms of verbs

Unit 46 introduced the idea of short forms in negative verbs. In this unit and the next unit, students practice other short forms of verbs.

1 Use the table in **1** for reference and to explain the difference between short and long forms. Point out that a few of the most common verbs in English have short forms. These short forms are very common in conversation. Short forms, or contractions, are also used in informal and personal writing, but are not generally used in formal written English (for example, academic papers and business letters).

You might point out to students that several of the verbs have identical short forms; for example, *'s* is the short form of both *is* and *has* while *'d* can be the short form of *had*, *would*, or *did*.

BACKGROUND

Most of these short forms are used only when the verb is an auxiliary. For example, the short form *'ve* could be used in place of *have* in *They have already paid* but not (at least in North American English) in *They have two children*. The short forms of the verb *be*, however, are used whether *be* is an auxiliary or main verb (for example, *You're joking* or *You're a good friend*).

The third column in the table gives the pronunciations of each of the short forms. The choice between varying pronunciations usually depends on what precedes the short form – for example, the short form of *would* (*'d*) would be pronounced /d/ in *I'd like to* but /ɪd/ (or /əd/) in *That'd be great*. The pronunciation of *have* as /ə/ occurs in rapid, informal speech after modal auxiliaries (for example, *You should have* /ʃʊdə/ *told me*). Note that the pronunciations of *'s* as the short form of *is* and *has* correspond to the three pronunciations for the grammatical *-s* ending, a topic which is dealt with in Unit 52.

The short form *'d* for *did* is probably more informal and less used than the other short forms given. It occurs mainly in questions after *where, why*, and so on.

2 Play the conversation through once and ask students just to listen. Then play it again, pausing at the end of each sentence to give students time to write their answers.

Answers

A: __I'd__ like some of those apples. How much __are they__ ?
B: __They're__ forty cents each. How many __would you__ like?
A: __I'll__ take five.
B: There __you are__ . Would you like a bag for them?
A: Yes, __I would__ . __My bag's__ full.
B: Anything else?
A: No, __that's__ all, thanks. How much __is that__ ?
B: __That'll__ be two dollars.
A: __Here's__ a twenty.
B: Have you got anything smaller?
A: Uh, __I'm__ not sure. No, __that's__ all __I've__ got.

3 During repetition and pairwork, make sure that students use the short forms where shown in the dialog.

EXTENSION

For **3**, in addition to or instead of practicing the conversation in **2**, students could work in pairs and write a similar conversation involving shopping. Selected pairs could then perform their conversations for the class, and other students could be asked to decide whether the pairs used short forms where appropriate.

---

4 Answers

1. The __long__ form of these verbs is used when the verb is the first or last word in a sentence. (Examples: *Have you got anything smaller?* and *Yes, I would.*)
2. The __long__ form is often used in questions beginning with a question word (such as *how*) when another word (such as *much* or *many*) comes after the question word. (Example: *How many would you like?*)

Note that these rules apply to the kinds of short forms in the table in **1**, not to negative short forms (which *can* be used at the beginning and end of sentences). For more information on where long forms rather than short forms are likely to occur, see *Background*, Unit 48, **2**.

5, 6 The short forms of *is, have, are,* and *will* and (in **6**) the negative forms of these verbs are practiced.

BACKGROUND

Short forms tend to be used in more contexts in speech than in writing. For example, short forms are common in speech after both nouns and pronouns; however, in writing, they are less likely to be used after nouns than after pronouns. Compare *Hannah's four* (spoken) versus *Hannah is four* (written). Words are often blended together in speech that would not necessarily be shown that way in writing. As another example, *what are* is likely to be blended in speech, but would probably not be represented as *what're* in writing. For more information about where short and long forms are likely to be used, see *Background* under 48, **2**. Other examples of blended forms that occur in spoken language but are not generally reflected in writing can be found in Part 5, especially Units 32 and 35.

7 As an alternative, students could describe the families of well-known people they know about.

UNIT 48 Weak forms of some pronouns; more on the long and short forms of verbs

BACKGROUND

In connected speech, personal pronouns are normally unstressed and pronounced with their weak forms.

Here are the strong and weak forms of the pronouns in the Student's Book.

	Strong form	Weak form
he	/hiy/	/i/ or /hi/
him	/hɪm/	/ɪm/ or /hɪm/
she	/ʃiy/	/ʃi/
her	/hər/	/ər/ or /hər/
it	/ɪt/	/ɪt/ or /ət/
they	/ðey/	/ðe/
them	/ðɛm/	/ðəm/ or /əm/
you	/yuw/	/yə/ or /yu/
your	/yʊr/ or /yɔr/	/yər/
my	/may/	(no commonly used distinct weak form)
we	/wiy/	/wi/

Note that not all pronouns here have the sound /ə/ in their weak forms. When pronouns like *he, she, they,* and *we* are unstressed, the vowel tends to be pronounced without the extra "glide" sound it often has in the strong forms of the pronouns (for more information, see *Background* in Unit 4), but is not usually reduced to /ə/.

Pronouns that begin with the letter *h* (for example, *he, him,* and *her*) often drop the /h/ sound in the weak form. They keep the /h/ sound, though, when the pronoun is at the beginning of a sentence or is given special emphasis. (There is more practice of pronouns beginning with *h* in Unit 37.) Note that the pronoun *them* may be reduced to /əm/ in rapid, informal speech, making it sound very close to the weak pronunciation of *him* as /ɪm/.

When pronouns within a sentence are pronounced with their weak forms, they are very often linked to and blended with the preceding word. This linking always occurs in the case of pronouns with a dropped /h/, so that, for example, *seen her* (sentence 9 in **1**) sounds like "seener" and *tell him* (sentence 10 in **1**) sounds like "tellim." When the pronouns *you* and *your* are blended with a preceding word that ends in the sound /t/, /d/, /s/, or /z/, palatalized forms like /dɪʤə/ for *did you* or /vɪzɪtʃər/ for *visit your* (sentence 5 in **1**) often result. (For more on palatalization, see Unit 35.)

1 Answers

1. I lost ___my___ wallet.
2. ___We___ all would.
3. ___He___ 's getting married.
4. ___It___ 's ten to five.
5. Let's visit ___your___ sister.
6. I put ___them___ on the table.
7. ___She___ 's five foot six.
8. Can't ___they___ take a cab?
9. I don't know. I haven't seen ___her___ lately.
10. I'll just tell ___him___ I already have plans.
11. I'm sorry. I tried to call ___you___ but ___your___ phone was busy.

The pronouns in the blanks are pronounced with their weak forms, except for *you* in sentence 11, which comes at the end of a clause and therefore has its strong form. Point out that not all the weak forms here have the sound /ə/. Notice, too, that sentence 5 uses the short form *'s* for the pronoun *us*.

2 Answers

a. 4	g. 6
b. 7	h. 9
c. 1	i. 10
d. 3	j. 2
e. 8	k. 5
f. 11	

You may want to point out questions in which the short form does or does not occur. In informal speech, it is quite common for short forms to immediately follow *wh-* words, though it is less common for these short forms to be shown in writing.

You could also ask what the long form of the verb is in the questions that use the short form. Note, for example, that the long form of *'s* is *is* in *What's the matter?* but *has* in *What's Eva been doing?*

BACKGROUND

The decision about when to use the long forms of *am, are, is, has, have, had, would, did,* and *will* rather than the short forms depends on various factors in addition to level of formality. Two rules were given in Unit 47: (1) the long form is used when the verb begins or ends a sentence, and (2) the long form is often used in questions beginning with *wh-* question words (*what, how,* and so on) when another word, such as *much,* follows the question word.

Notice also that short forms are less likely to be used if the preceding sound is identical or very similar to the sound of the short form. For example, the short form *'d* for *would* is much more likely to occur in *Who'd like to come?* (item j), after the vowel in *who,* than in *What would you like to do?* (item k), after the /t/ in *what.* After *where,* the short form *'re* for *are* seems much less likely to occur than, for example, the short form *'ve* for *have* (compare items g, *Where are the tickets?,* and f, *Where've you been?*). The short form *'s* is common after *that,* but not after *this.* In general, short forms seem less likely to occur where they would need to be pronounced as a separate syllable (for example, *these're*). Sentence rhythm probably also plays a role: You might say *What time's your train?* but not *What time's it?*

For detailed information on short forms and where they are used in speech and writing, as well as on blended forms that are not represented in writing, see C. Hill and L. Beebe "Contraction and Blending: The Use of Orthographic Clues in Teaching Pronunciation" in *TESOL Quarterly* (1980), Vol. XIV, No. 3.

4 Listening script

Police officer: Police Department, Sergeant Connolly speaking. How can I help you?

Mrs. Valdez: I'm calling to report a missing person – two missing people – my children.

Officer: What are their names?

Mrs. Valdez: Alex and Chris Valdez.

Officer: How old are they, Mrs. Valdez?

Mrs. Valdez: Alex is eight and Chris is ten.

Officer: And how long have they been missing?

Mrs. Valdez: They went to the park at two o'clock. They've been gone for over three hours.

Officer: Can you describe them? What were they wearing?

Mrs. Valdez: Well, Alex was wearing her green shorts and Chris has jeans on, I think. They're both wearing T-shirts, and I think Chris has a jacket with him. Let's see . . . she has blond hair, and he has dark hair – oh, but he's probably wearing a hat.

Officer: Anything else you can tell me about them?

Mrs. Valdez: Uh, they've got their dog with them. And . . . oh, thank goodness . . . they just walked through the door.

Answers

Picture b shows Alex, and picture d shows Chris.

5, 6 Encourage students to use short forms of verbs and weak forms of pronouns in their descriptions.

7 Compare the pronunciation of the strong forms of these pronouns with the way they are often said in relaxed speech when combined with the short form *'ll*:

I /ay/	I'll /ɑl/	(rhymes with *doll*)
you /yuw/	you'll /yʊl/	(rhymes with *pull*)
he /hiy/	he'll /hɪl/	(sounds like *hill*)
she /ʃiy/	she'll /ʃɪl/	(rhymes with *hill*)
we /wiy/	we'll /wɪl/	(sounds like *will*)
they /ðey/	they'll /ðɛl/	(rhymes with *bell*)

Point out the rhyming or sound-alike words to students.

UNIT 49 Weak forms of some conjunctions

1 Answers

1. a. Milk __but__ no sugar.
   b. Milk __and__ no sugar.
2. a. July __and__ August.
   b. July __or__ August.
3. a. It was small __but__ very heavy.
   b. It was small __and__ very heavy.

4. a. Amy __and__ her friend.
   b. Amy __or__ her friend.
5. a. __But__ I want to go.
   b. __And__ I want to go.
6. a. Red __or__ green.
   b. Red __and__ green.

2 During repetition, make sure that students use the weak pronunciations of the words in the spaces: *and* /ən/ (as in *July and August*) or /n/ (as in *Red and green*); *or* /ər/; and *but* /bət/. These words are normally said with their weak forms. (There is more practice of the weak form of *and* in Part 4, Unit 28, and practice of the weak forms of *and* and *or* in Part 5, Unit 32.)

3 Demonstrate the activity first with a student before students work in pairs.

4 Listening script

1. In January, Washington is colder than Mexico City.
2. In July, Montreal is as wet as Washington.
3. In July, Seattle is sunnier than Miami.
4. In January, Miami is about as sunny as Los Angeles.
5. In July, Washington is hotter than Mexico City.
6. In January, Seattle is about the same temperature as Montreal.
7. In January, Montreal is colder than Washington.
8. In July, Mexico City is sunnier than Los Angeles.

Answers

1. T   2. T   3. F   4. T   5. T   6. F   7. T   8. F

The words *as* and *than* are usually said with their weak forms (that is, with the unstressed vowel /ə/). The strong form of *as* (/æz/) may be used in certain phrases, including *as is*, *as of*, and *as for*.

5 Demonstrate the activity first with a student. During pairwork, monitor the weak forms of *as* and *than*, which are both pronounced with the unstressed vowel /ə/.

EXTENSION

1. You could do a similar task to that in **5**, using information the students have gathered about each other comparing such features as height, weight, age, and so on.
2. Use similes as a context for further practice of the weak form of *as*. For example, have students work in pairs to decide which of the animals best completes each comparison (the answers are given in parentheses below):

a bird	a mouse	a bear	a fox	a mule
a lamb	a kitten	a pig	an ox	a peacock

1. as gentle as (a lamb)
2. as hungry as (a bear)
3. as weak as (a kitten)
4. as free as (a bird)
5. as stubborn as (a mule)
6. as strong as (an ox)
7. as sly as (a fox)
8. as quiet as (a mouse)
9. as proud as (a peacock)
10. as fat as (a pig)

Point out that these are common similes in English. Then ask students if they have similar expressions in their native languages.

UNIT 50 Weak and strong forms of some prepositions

1 Answers

1. for/at
2. at/from
3. from/to
4. from/of
5. at/to
6. for/from
7. from/of
8. at/to

2 Answers

1. He was looking for the children in the park.
2. I was home at six o'clock.
3. They drove from Portland last night.
4. He had a drawing of Rome.
5. She picked up the ball and threw it at her brother.
6. Do you like this picture? It's a present for Sarah.
7. The people of France drink a lot of wine.
8. She pointed to the ship.

The prepositions in **2** are all said with their weak forms.

3 You may want to point out that you need to say the weak forms within a phrase or sentence. If you say a preposition by itself, it will be stressed and have its strong form.

Note that *to* can have a weak form /tu/ when it occurs before a vowel (for example, *to England*). This pronunciation is not shown in the table. Although *to* is traditionally described as having the weak form /tə/ before a consonant and the weak form /tu/ or /tʊ/ before a vowel, many native speakers ignore this distinction, using /tə/ before both vowels and consonants.

Both strong and weak forms of *from* and *of* are shown with the same symbol /ə/ but the strong forms use the full, stressed vowel /ə/ (as in *bus*), while the weak forms use reduced, unstressed /ə/ (as in *across*).

4 The completed sentences in **1** are recorded again here. During repetition, monitor the pronunciation of *at, for, from, of,* and *to,* and offer correction if these words are not pronounced with the unstressed sound /ə/ (schwa).

5 Answers

1. S	6. W
2. W	7. S, S
3. W	8. S
4. S	9. W
5. S	10. S

Try to elicit from students that the strong form is used: (1) when the preposition ends a sentence (examples 1, 4, 5, 8, and 10), and (2) when a preposition is intended to contrast with another preposition (example 7).

7 Listening script

From my home in Bar Harbor, first I'm going to Boston, in the eastern part of Massachusetts. In Boston, I'm going to stay at the Beacon Guest House. I'll stay there for two days. Then I'm going to drive from Boston to New York City. I'm planning to stay at the Stage Hotel in New York for four days. From New York, I'm going to drive to Philadelphia and stay at the Liberty Hotel for one night. Then I'm going to drive to Washington, D.C. I'll stay at the Capital Hotel for two days. From Washington, I'm going to drive to Niagara Falls, on the border of the U.S. and Canada. I'm going to stay at the Rainbow Motel for two days. After that, I'll drive home again.

In addition to the weak forms of prepositions, notice the pronunciation of *going to* as "gonna" (/gənə/ or /gɔnə/) when used with future meaning before a verb (as in *I'm going to drive to Philadelphia*, not as in *I'm going to Boston*). There is more on this blended form in Unit 32.

8 The starting point for the planned trip could be anywhere in the eastern part of the United States. If students are in the eastern U.S., then the starting point could be the place where they live. Or they could imagine that they are arriving in the United States by air.

You may find it useful to demonstrate this activity first. Point out that students should use language similar to the language in the example on the recording (*I'm going to . . ., to drive to . . ., to drive from . . .to . . ., to stay at . . ., for . . . days,* and so on). This will provide plenty of opportunity to use prepositions. During pairwork, monitor the pronunciation of the prepositions *at, for, from, of,* and *to.*

UNIT 51 Pronouncing -ed endings

1 Listening script

Note that verbs ending in -ed are underlined.

Jane Garfield: I saw a terrible accident last week.
Friend: Why, what <u>happened</u>?
Jane Garfield: Well, I was working in my office. I <u>wanted</u> to see what the weather was like, so I <u>walked</u> over to the window and <u>looked</u> outside.
Friend: And what did you see?
Jane Garfield: Well, nothing at first. But then a car came down the road. It <u>stopped</u> at the intersection opposite my office. A man and a woman <u>started</u> to cross when another car drove straight through the intersection without even slowing down.
Friend: Oh, no! Was anybody hurt?
Jane Garfield: Well, the woman <u>jumped</u> out of the way and the car just <u>missed</u> her. But it <u>knocked</u> down the man.
Friend: So what did you do?
Jane Garfield: Well, after that I <u>called</u> for an ambulance and the police and then I went outside.
Friend: Did it take long for them to come?
Jane Garfield: No, they <u>arrived</u> in just, oh, maybe two or three minutes. The ambulance workers <u>helped</u> the woman to stand up. I think she was OK. But they <u>carried</u> the man into the ambulance on a stretcher. I <u>explained</u> what I'd seen to the police.
Friend: And what about the driver?
Jane Garfield: Well, apparently they found the man and <u>arrested</u> him.

Answer

The headline *Man Injured by Car at Intersection* best summarizes what happened.

3 Answers

/t/	/d/	/ɪd/
walked	explained	wanted
knocked	called	arrested
jumped	arrived	started
looked	carried	
stopped		
helped		
missed		

4 Direct attention to the types of sounds listed in each column. The most important thing to note – more important than where /t/ and /d/ each occur – is that the *-ed* ending is pronounced as a separate syllable only after the sounds in the third column. Only the sound /t/ (as in *arrested*) is now shown in the third column; /d/ (as in *needed*) will be added later.

Point out the change in spelling when *-ed* is added to a word like *carry*. In verbs that end with a consonant followed by the letter *y*, the *y* is changed to *i* before adding *-ed* (and the ending is pronounced /d/).

BACKGROUND

The rules for pronouncing *-ed* endings are as follows:

1. It is pronounced /ɪd/ (or /əd/) after verbs that end with /t/ or /d/.
2. It is pronounced /t/ after /p/, /k/, /f/, /θ/, /s/, /ʃ/, and /tʃ/ (voiceless consonants other than /t/).
3. It is pronounced /d/ after all other sounds (i.e., vowels and voiced consonants other than /d/).

These rules are somewhat of a simplification, since the linking that occurs in connected speech can affect the pronunciation of the final /t/ or /d/ sound. And remember that final voiced consonants may not sound strongly voiced, especially when followed by a voiceless consonant or silence. Often, the clearest indication that a final consonant is voiced is the lengthening of a preceding vowel (for more on this, see the notes for Unit 9).

5 After students hear the story again, this task could be done in a number of ways. One way is for students to close their books and attempt to retell the story without the prompts and words given. You could ask one student to start and when this student has contributed some of the story, ask another to continue. Alternatively, ask students to retell the story making use of the prompts and words. Then, at a later stage – maybe at the end of the lesson or on a following day – ask them to try to retell it from memory without the prompts and words. Another possibility is for students to work in pairs and for one to retell the story to a partner. Choose a method (or methods) appropriate for your class.

Answers

The verbs to be written in the spaces are underlined (and appear in the same order) in the listening script in **1**. Note, however, that the first verb, *happened*, is not used in **5**.

7 Answers

1. rained
2. dropped
3. polluted
4. arrived, mailed
5. finished
6. passed
7. laughed
8. decided
9. washed
10. walked

BACKGROUND

Most of the verbs to be filled for in **7** either end the sentence or are followed by a vowel. This highlights the three pronunciations of -ed, avoiding any changes in their pronunciation caused by contact with a following consonant. Items 4 and 7, however, contain -ed verbs followed by a consonant: *arrived yet* and *laughed the*. For information on the kinds of changes that occur in cases like these, see **4** through **7** of this unit; the *Background* for Unit 34; **6**, also in Unit 34; and Unit 35, *Background* for **7** through **9**. For a detailed description of these changes, see the article by Mary S. Temperley, "Linking and Deletion in Final Consonant Clusters," in Morley (1987, pp. 63–82), in the list of recommended books in To the Teacher.

Note that the adjective *tired*, in item 10, follows the same pronunciation rules as the verbs in the box. Most -ed adjectives follow these rules. However, some do not, and add an extra syllable regardless of what consonant sound precedes the -ed; for example, *crooked*, *wretched*, *wicked*, and *rugged*.

9 Answers

Additions to the table are listed below:

/t/	/d/	/ɪd/
/f/ lau**gh**ed /ʃ/ fini**sh**ed, wa**sh**ed		/d/ deci**d**ed

EXTENSION

Ask students to find more past tense -ed words (for example, in other textbooks) and to decide how the ending is pronounced. They can add sounds/letters to the table where necessary.

10 To add a competitive element, count the number of words used in each story that end in -ed. Students should try to use the maximum number possible while keeping the story coherent. You could set a time limit, too.

At the end, select students to report their stories to the class. You could ask other students to monitor the pronunciation of past tense -ed endings during the story telling.

11 Listening script

The following example story is on the recording:

One day Daniel woke up, looked at the clock, and realized that he was late for work. He washed, shaved, and brushed his teeth. He hurried downstairs. Because he was late, he skipped breakfast. He walked quickly to the bus stop. He waited for about five minutes until the bus arrived. But when he got to his office, he discovered that it was closed. Suddenly he remembered that it was Sunday!

UNIT 52 Pronouncing -s endings

1 Explain that what is important for deciding how to pronounce the -s ending is the sound, not the spelling, at the end of the noun or verb. For example, both *take* and *book* end with the sound /k/, even though one word has a final *e* in the spelling. With both these words, therefore, the -s ending is pronounced the same way – as /s/. And in both *catches* and *Mitch's*, the ending is pronounced /ɪz/, because the sound before it is /tʃ/, even though the ending is spelled -es in one word and 's in the other.

BACKGROUND

The rules for pronouncing the -s (-es) ending are as follows:

1. It is pronounced /ɪz/ (or /əz/) after /s/, /z/, /ʃ/, /ʒ/, /tʃ/, and /dʒ/.
2. It is pronounced /s/ after /p/, /t/, /k/, /f/, and /θ/ (voiceless consonants other than /s/, /ʃ/, /tʃ/).
3. It is pronounced /z/ after all other sounds.

2 Answers

The odd one out in each line is as follows:

1. runs /z/ (The others end in /s/.)
2. includes /z/ (The others end in /ɪz/.)
3. loses /ɪz/ (The others end in /z/.)
4. gets /s/ (The others end in /z/.)
5. touches /ɪz/ (The others end in /s/.)
6. promises /ɪz/ (The others end in /z/.)
7. Jeff's /s/ (The others end in /z/.)

3 Answers

/s/	/z/	/ɪz/
/k/ /p/ /t/ /f/ (spelled *f* or *gh*)	/n/ /d/ /l/ /v/ /ŋ/ (spelled *ng*) /r/ /m/ /b/ (vowel sound)	/ʃ/ (spelled *sh*) /z/ /s/ /tʃ/ (spelled *ch* or *tch*)

The ending -es is pronounced as a separate syllable only after the sounds shown in the third column (sounds made with a "hissing" noise).

Stop the recording after each word to give students time to repeat and to write a letter or symbol in the table. Alternatively, you could wait until students have repeated all the words before asking them to write the sounds in the table.

As with the -*ed* ending, it is much more important for students to know when to add – and especially when not to add – a separate syllable for the -*s* ending than to be overly concerned with the distinction between the /s/ and /z/ pronunciations. (See *Background* under Unit 51, **4**.) Explain or elicit the rules: add voiceless /s/ after most voiceless sounds, voiced /z/ after most voiced sounds, and an extra syllable /ɪz/ (or /əz/) after consonants made with a hissing noise (sibilants like /s/ and affricates like /tʃ/).

You may want to point out that the presence of an *e* before the final *s* does not necessarily mean that the ending is pronounced as a separate syllable. There is an extra syllable only if the *e* is added to the spelling when the ending is attached (as in <u>*catches*</u>), not if the *e* is part of the base word (as in <u>*gloves*</u>). With possessive nouns, of course, no *e* is added, even where the ending is pronounced /ɪz/.

5 Answers

The following additions should be made: /g/ under /z/ (as in *bags*) and /dʒ/ (spelled *dg* here, in *bridges*) under /ɪz/.

6 Check that students can produce the correct questions. To do this, have them ask you the questions first and, if necessary, write the questions on the board (for example, *Do you like old movies?*). Students will need to stand up and walk around the room to do this activity.

PART 8   *Pronouncing written words*

INTRODUCTION

Aims and organization

In Part 8, students learn about some of the connections between pronunciation and written letters. The rules that connect sounds and spellings in English are complex. In Part 8, students are introduced to some rules that are fairly easy to understand and remember.

Unit 53   Letters and sounds (shows that the number of letters and sounds in a word may be different; also shows that consonant letters usually represent only one sound and gives practice in identifying consonants at the beginnings of words)

Unit 54   Pronouncing consonant letters: *c* and *g*

Unit 55   Pronouncing *th*

Unit 56   Pronouncing *sh*, *ch*, and *gh*; other spellings for /ʃ/ and /ʧ/ (first focuses on common ways that the consonant pairs *sh*, *ch*, and *gh* are pronounced and then on contexts in which the letters *t* and *c* often represent the sounds /ʃ/ and /ʧ/)

Unit 57   Pronunciation, spelling, and word stress (identifying and spelling the unstressed vowel sound /ə/ [as in a̲cross])

Unit 58   Pronouncing single vowel letters: *a, e, i, o,* and *u*

Unit 59   Pronouncing vowel pairs: (*oa, ei, ee, oo, ea,* and *ou*)

Unit 60   Silent letters (letters that are not pronounced)

General notes

Some recommended sources of information on sound-spelling relationships include the following: A. C. Gimson's *An Introduction to the Pronunciation of English* (Edward Arnold, 1989) lists possible spellings of each of the sounds of English together with example words. C. Prator and B. Robinett's *Manual of American English Pronunciation* (Harcourt Brace, 1985, Lessons 17 and 18) gives detailed information on sound-spelling relationships for vowels, including a useful table showing regular and irregular spelling patterns. M. Celce-Murcia, D. Brinton, and J. Goodwin's, *Teaching Pronunciation* (Cambridge University Press, 1996, Chapter 9) describes a number of spelling rules, including discussion of more complicated sound-spelling relationships and silent letters. W. B. Dickerson's *Stress in the Speech Stream: The Rhythm of Spoken English* (University of Illinois Press, 1989) gives detailed information and exercises on predicting sounds from spellings, especially in longer words. J. Kenworthy's *Teaching English Pronunciation* (Longman, 1987, Chapter 5) gives a brief introduction to the English spelling system, a concise set of rules for the pronunciation of English letters, and some suggestions for teaching.

UNIT 53 Letters and sounds

1 This activity calls attention to the fact that the number of sounds in a word often differs from the number of letters.

Answers

dog S	window D	not S
luck D	she D	thin D
cough D	chess D	mix D
cats S	bill D	other D
plan S	most S	young D

2 Monitor the pronunciation of the words during repetition.

EXTENSION

Ask students to decide how many letters and how many sounds are in each word in **1**. The answers are as follows:

	Number of			Number of	
	letters	sounds		letters	sounds
dog	3	3	bill	4	3
luck	4	3	most	4	4
cough	5	3	not	3	3
cats	4	4	thin	4	3
plan	4	4	mix	3	4
window	6	5	other	5	4
she	3	2	young	5	3
chess	5	3			

3 Answers

b	1	g	2	m	1	s	2
c	2	h	1	n	1	t	1
d	1	k	1	p	1	v	1
f	1	l	1	r	1	w	1

Three consonant letters have two common pronunciations:

1. The letter *c* can be pronounced /k/ (*car*) or /s/ (*police*).
2. The letter *g* can be pronounced /g/ (*green*) or /dʒ/ (*age*).
3. The letter *s* can be pronounced /s/ (*swim*) or /z/ (*visit*).

4   This is an "around-the-class" activity. Point out that the last *letter* of each word is the same as the first letter of the next, and then ask for ways of continuing the chain given in the Student's Book. Make sure that students realize that they need to think about spellings rather than sounds. Start a new chain by giving a word yourself and asking for a suggestion for the next word. Continue to ask for suggestions as the chain grows, or call on students. A student who gives a wrong word or a repeated word is eliminated. Keep a note of words that cause problems, and at the end check that students can pronounce them correctly.

UNIT 54   Pronouncing consonant letters: *c* and *g*

The spellings dealt with in this unit are traditionally known as *hard c* and *g* (pronounced /k/ and /g/, respectively) and *soft c* and *g* (pronounced /s/ and /dʒ/).

1, 2   Answers

The traffic is bad in the center of the city.

I had a cup of coffee at a cafe.

I've been to South America twice.

Only take this medicine in an emergency.

I went across the street to the post office.

I can't decide what courses to take.

I haven't had a cigarette since December.

Call the police!

4   Answer

The letter *c* is pronounced /s/ before the letters   e   ,   i   , or   y   in a word, and it is pronounced /k/ everywhere else.

EXTENSION

If relevant for your students, show them that the rules for pronouncing *c* can help them with the pronunciation of related words like the following (also see Unit 27, for help with predicting stress in words like these): *produce – production, reduce – reduction; medicine – medical; electric – electricity, public – publicity, authentic – authenticity; critic – criticize.*

---

5 Answers

good-bye   <u>together</u>   grandparents   stranger   bag   <u>girl</u>
cigarette   magic   dangerous   again   <u>begin</u>   Egypt
grass   <u>give</u>   engine   change   <u>get</u>   large   language
register   vegetables   Germany   <u>forget</u>

7 Students should monitor one another's pronunciation of the letter *g*.

EXTENSION

Ask students for other words that contain either the letter *c* or the letter *g*. List them on the board and tell students to group them into (1) words that follow the rules given in this unit and (2) exceptions.

UNIT 55   Pronouncing *th*

BACKGROUND

Relevant rules for the pronunciation of *th* are as follows:

1. At the beginning of words *th* is pronounced /θ/ (as in <u>th</u>ink) except in some common grammar words; these include *the, they, them, their, this, that, these, those, than, then, there,* and *though*.
2. At the ends of words *th* is nearly always pronounced /θ/; examples include *bath, path, month, mouth, north, south,* and *tooth* (exceptions: *smooth* and, for many speakers, *with*).
3. When *th* comes in the middle of a word, a useful rule (though one with exceptions) is that it is pronounced /ð/ in words where it comes before an *-er* ending (for example, *mother, father, brother, either, together, weather, other*) and /θ/ when it does not (for example, *author, athlete, sympathy, nothing, mathematics, method, cathedral*).

1 Answers

How many are there?	A thousand.
What's the matter?	I'm thirsty.
Is this yours?	Yes. Thank you.
What time is their train?	Three thirty.
Where are they?	Through here.
Is he heavier than me?	No, he's thinner.
What day will you be there?	On Thursday.

3 Monitor the pronunciation of *th* during repetition and practice in pairs.

4 Answer

At the beginning of a word, *th* is normally pronounced / ð / in grammar words (such as *the, they, them, that,* and *there*) and / θ / in other kinds of words.

Point out that this rule applies to the consonant pair *th* only at the *beginning* of words.

EXTENSION

To help students see how the rule in **4** is applied, ask them to think of more grammar words that begin with *th* and that are pronounced /ð/. (See the list under *Background* at the beginning of this unit.)

---

5 Answer

When *th* is at the end of a word, it is usually pronounced / θ /.

Note that *smooth* and (for many people) *with* are exceptions to this rule. Also note that when *-s* is added to form the plural of some words ending in *th* (for example, *path* or *mouth*), the *th* may be pronounced /ð/ rather than /θ/.

EXTENSION

You could show students that while *th* at the end of a word is usually pronounced /θ/, the spelling *the* at the end of a word is pronounced /ð/. You could give students practice with pairs of related nouns and verbs that illustrate this rule (note that these pairs may include a difference in the sound of the vowel, too). Examples include: *breath/breathe, bath/bathe, teeth/teethe,* and *cloth/clothe*.

---

6 Answers

<u>father</u>   bathroom   nothing   <u>other</u>   <u>weather</u>   birthday
something   <u>together</u>   authority   <u>either</u>   <u>rather</u>   healthy

In the middle of a word, *th* is usually pronounced /ð/ if the word ends in   *er*   .

8 Answers

Joseph Stalin died: March 5, 1953
Bill Clinton became President of the United States: January 20, 1993
The first soccer World Cup was played in Uruguay: July 13, 1930
Hong Kong was returned to China: June 30, 1997
The first modern Olympic Games began in Athens, Greece: April 6, 1896
The Wright brothers flew the first airplane: December 17, 1903

If you think your students may be unsure about how to say the dates, have them practice saying them first, before working in groups.

9 Monitor /θ/ and /ð/ pronunciations when students discuss their answers. The sound /θ/ occurs frequently in the dates here (for example, *July thir<u>teenth</u>, nineteen <u>thirty</u>*).

EXTENSION

You can provide practice of /θ/ with almost any activity in which students are required to give dates. For example, you could ask students, for homework, to look up the birthdates of some famous people and to report back during another class. Or you could simply ask students to give their own date of birth.

More practice of /θ/ and /ð/ can be found in Units 11 and 12.

Unit 56 Pronouncing *sh, ch,* and *gh*; other spellings for /ʃ/ and /tʃ/

BACKGROUND

Relevant information on the pronunciation of *sh, ch,* and *gh* is as follows:

1. The consonant pair *sh* is always pronounced /ʃ/ (for example, *ship*).
2. The consonant pair *ch* is usually pronounced /tʃ/. It is almost always pronounced this way after the letter *t* (for example, *match, kitchen*) and at the end of a word (for example, *rich, each*). It can also be pronounced /k/ (*chemistry, character, architect*) and /ʃ/ (*machine*).
3. The consonant pair *gh* can be pronounced /g/ (*ghost*) or /f/ (*rough*), or it can be silent after the letter *i* (*high*) and some other vowels (*through*).

1 Answers

1. one
2. machine, stomach
3. *Possible answers:* tough, rough, cough, laugh
4. *Possible answers:* night, high
5. ghost

Note that *stomach* is an exception to the rule given under *Background* about the pronunciation of *ch* at the end of a word.

3 Answers

The following are the most likely answers:

1. cheese, fish
2. shoes, shirt
3. shampoo, toothbrush
4. washing machine, dishwasher
5. shiver, cough

6. chest, stomach
7. ship, fish
8. Chinese, French
9. tough, fresh
10. rough, sharp

5

To make the task a little easier, give some key words to help students write the sentences. There are various possibilities. Here are some:

1. When . . . walk?
2. How . . . pay?
3. Why . . . call me?
4. What . . . get?
5. Why . . . so hungry?

6 Answers

	/ʃ/	/tʃ/			/ʃ/	/tʃ/
1. information	☑	☐	9. special		☑	☐
2. furniture	☐	☑	10. commercial		☑	☐
3. education	☑	☐	11. temperature		☐	☑
4. tissue	☑	☐	12. examination		☑	☐
5. suggestion	☐	☑	13. natural		☐	☑
6. profession	☑	☐	14. delicious		☑	☐
7. question	☐	☑	15. national		☑	☐
8. musician	☑	☐	16. actual		☐	☑

8 Answers

	/ʃ/	/tʃ/			/ʃ/	/tʃ/
1. future	☐	☑	4. official		☑	☐
2. discussion	☑	☐	5. position		☑	☐
3. conversation	☑	☐	6. picture		☐	☑

EXTENSION

After students check their answers in **9**, you could ask them to complete each of these rules with the correct symbol, /ʃ/ (*shoe*) or /tʃ/ (*cheese*).

At the beginning of many *unstressed* syllables spelled with *i* (followed by another vowel) or *u* (followed by *r* or a vowel):

1. The letter *t* is pronounced / / in *tu* and in *sti*.
2. The underlined letters are pronounced / /: *ci*, *ti*, *ssi*, *ssu*.

After students answer (1. /tʃ/; 2. /ʃ/), you could ask for example words.

UNIT 57 Pronunciation, spelling, and word stress

BACKGROUND

Students often expect a sound to be associated with a particular spelling. The variety of spellings for unstressed /ə/ and /ər/ can be a major source of student difficulty with these sounds. For example, students may think that /ər/ is spelled only as *er*, and when they see a spelling like *ar* they may use the vowel /ɑ/.

For more information on the pronunciation of vowels in unstressed syllables, see the notes for Part 4, Unit 26.

1 The underlined letters are pronounced as unstressed /ə/. For information about the sound /ə/, see the notes for Units 2 and 26.

2 Answers

○	○	○	○	○	○
across	problem	magazine	tomorrow	probably	profession

○	○	○	○	○	○
curious	instrument	suggest	animal	common	committee

Note that *magazine* can be pronounced with strong stress on the first or last syllable. It is said on the recording with stress on the first syllable.

3 During repetition, monitor the pronunciation of /ə/ in the words. Point out or elicit from students that /ə/ is a very common vowel in *unstressed* syllables. Notice that in pairs of words like *probably* and *profession*, *common* and *committee*, the vowel in the first syllable is pronounced /ə/ if the syllable is not stressed. If the syllable is stressed, the vowel has a different pronunciation.

4 Answers

Spelling	Examples
a	across, magazine, probably, animal
e	problem, instrument
i	animal
o	tomorrow, profession, common, committee
ou	curious
u	instrument, suggest

5 Answers

daughter   doctor   percent   pleasure   regular   yesterday
neighbor   forward   forgot   modern   information

Spellings for the sound /ər/ include: *er, or, ure, ar.*

More information on the pronunciation of /ər/ can be found in Units 8 and 26.

Pronouncing written words / Part 8

6 Answer

Schwa is the most common vowel sound in   unstressed   syllables.

Notice that schwa is especially common in the syllable *next to* a stressed syllable.

EXTENSION

Ask more advanced students "Are all unstressed vowels pronounced as schwa?"

Prompt them to notice that not all unstressed vowels are pronounced as /ə/. You could direct attention to words used in this lesson or to other words students know to help them answer the question. For example, the last syllables in *tomorrow, probably,* and *committee* are unstressed, but the vowels are not pronounced as /ə/. The second syllable in *curious* is also unstressed, but the vowel is pronounced as /i/ rather than /ə/. All these are words from the box in **2** in the Student's Book. Other examples include: *city, happy, hotel, narrow, pronunciation.*

---

7 Answers

The following are possible answers. The vowels pronounced as unstressed /ə/ are underlined.

accident (or accident); ambulance; ambulance workers; apartment building; bus driver; camera; children; corner; gas station; helmet; intersection; jacket; ladder; motorcycle (or motorcycle); movie theater; newspaper; passengers; pedestrian; person (or people); photographer; police officer/policeman; stretcher; supermarket; telephone; uniform; woman/women

Note that sometimes (as in *accident*) an unstressed vowel might be said as either /ə/ or /ɪ/. The last syllables of *station, intersection, motorcycle, person,* and *people* and the second syllable of *passengers* could be considered to have either /ə/ or a syllabic consonant.

EXTENSION

To give more practice with vowels pronounced as /ə/, ask students to copy a sentence down from one of their textbooks. Tell them to try to predict which vowels will be pronounced as unstressed /ə/ by underlining them. Then they listen to you saying the sentence or to a recording of it so that they can check their predictions.

UNIT 58 Pronouncing single vowel letters

This unit presents some rules for pronouncing single vowel letters and deciding whether these should be said with their *name sound*, with their *base sound*, or as /ə/ (schwa). The terms *name* and *base* correspond to the more traditional terms *long* and *short*. The terms *name sound* and *base sound* are used here instead of the more traditional terms to try to avoid misunderstandings that arise when students think that the main distinction between long and short vowels is in length rather than sound quality. Note that the unit is rather long and presents several rules. You may want to break it up into two lessons.

2 Answers

USA = the United States of America   CIA = Central Intelligence Agency
UN = the United Nations   UFO = Unidentified Flying Object
CEO = Chief Executive Officer   IOU = I owe you
VIP = Very Important Person   ESL = English as a Second Language

Monitor the pronunciation of the abbreviations, which are all said with the names of the letters. Note that abbreviations like these are typically said with prominence on the last letter.

3 Answers

<u>cake</u>	fact	<u>life</u>	tap	cup	left	<u>home</u>
<u>these</u>	bit	<u>cute</u>	spell	bag	drop	
<u>tape</u>	smile	<u>rule</u>	soft	<u>nose</u>	kill	dust

5 Answers

Vowel	-VCe	-VC(C)
a	cake, tape	fact, tap, bag
e	these	left, spell
i	life, smile	bit, kill
o	home, nose	drop, soft
u	cute, rule	cup, dust

Ask students to complete the table. Explain that V = a vowel letter (either *a, e, i, o,* or *u*), C = a consonant letter, and e = the letter *e*. For example, *home* is CVCe, *soft* is CVCC, and *cup* is CVC. The symbol (C) means that a consonant sound might or might not occur. To complete the table, students need to look only at the first vowel in the words in **3** and the letters that follow it. So, for example, *home* fits under -VCe, and *soft* and *cup* under -VC(C).

6 Answer

When the written form of a one-syllable word ends with __VCe__ (or Ce – i.e., a single consonant followed by the letter e), the first vowel letter is usually pronounced with its name.

Direct Students to fill in the blank with a spelling pattern (see the column headings in the table in **5** or the patterns shown in the box at **8**). The letter e, though less precise, could also be accepted as an answer.

EXTENSION

1. One group of words that does not always follow the rule in **6** is given in the Student's Book. There are other exceptions, too. Give students a list of words like the following: *are, drive, some, none, case, Rome, lose, have, move, bone, give, done, were, home, five, come, live, save.* Have students work in pairs. Ask them to underline the words that do *not* follow the rule given in **6**. Then read the words aloud (or have them on a recording), so that students can repeat the words and check their answers. Note that words that break the rule often end in *me, ne, re, se* (as well as *ve*).

2. As an additional exercise, ask students if the rule in **6** also applies to one-syllable words in which the vowel is followed by *two* consonant letters + the letter e. Either ask them to provide examples or give them some; for example, *bridge, dance, else, France, edge, horse, large, nurse, once, since, sense.* Note that the rule does not normally apply in such cases, but there are a few exceptions that do follow the rule given; for example, *change, taste,* and *waste*.

---

8 Answer

When the written form of a one-syllable word ends with __VC__ or __VCC__, the vowel letter is usually pronounced with its base sound.

Note that the word *soft* in the table in **5** will be an exception to the rule for those North American speakers who pronounce this word with the vowel /ɔ/ rather than /ɑ/.

In addition to the types of exceptions mentioned in the Student's Book, a number of words ending in the spelling oCC (for example, *gold, most, old,* and *roll*) or iCC (for example, *child, find,* and *high*) are pronounced with their name sound rather than base sound.

9 Answers

1. minute S
2. suppose N
3. purpose S
4. confuse N
5. interrupt B

6. assistant S
7. private S
8. accurate S
9. relate N
10. encourage S

11. represent B
12. frequent S
13. determine S
14. define N

You may want to summarize the rules students need to apply on the board. For example:

If stressed: 1. -VCe: vowel has its name sound.
                   2. -VC(C): vowel has its base sound.
If unstressed: vowel has the sound /ə/.

There are, of course, exceptions to these rules (for example, the vowels in the last syllable of *police, machine,* and *above* are not pronounced with their name sounds). But the rules given are intended to help students, for example, avoid overgeneralizing the rule in **6** to apply to all words rather than just one-syllable words and stressed final syllables. There is more practice of unstressed vowels in Units 26 and 57.

11   In all the words in the box, the vowel in the first syllable has its base sound.

As with other spelling rules, there are exceptions to the rule for pronouncing VCC; for example: *soldier, island, poster, tasted, other, nothing, wonder, only,* and words where *r* follows the vowel.

EXTENSION

To help students see how the VCC rule is applied when adding a common ending, tell students, *When you add* -ing *to a word like* plan, *you double the last consonant:* planning. Ask them if they can explain why. Then ask them in which of the following words they would double the last consonant before adding -ing: *swim, feel, shop, admit, happen, smile.*

Answer: When you add -ing to a word like *plan,* you double the last consonant because the VCC spelling in the stressed syllable shows that the vowel is pronounced with its base sound. You would double the last consonant before adding -ing in: *swim, shop, admit.*

---

12 Answers

The following are possible answers:

There are twenty nickels in a dollar.
Doctors often work in hospitals.
Moscow is the capital of Russia.
Summer and winter are both seasons.
You wear sandals and slippers on your feet.
Broccoli is a vegetable closely related to cabbage.
It generally costs less to mail a letter than a package.
Plastic and rubber are both materials.

UNIT 59 Pronouncing vowel pairs

1 Answers

The following are the most likely answers:

1. three	5. between	9. eighteen	13. school
2. spoon	6. cheap	10. sleep	14. eat
3. wool	7. afternoon	11. easy	15. already
4. clean	8. cooking	12. heavy	16. break

3 Answers

	/iy/ (piece)	/ey/ (day)	/uw/ (June)	/ɛ/ (red)	/ʊ/ (put)
ee	three, between, eighteen, sleep				
oo			spoon, afternoon, school		wool, cooking
ea	clean, cheap, easy, eat	break		heavy, already	

Note that the spelling *ee* normally represents the sound /iy/ (exception: *been*). The spelling *oo* typically represents the sound /uw/ before most letters, though it usually represents the sound /ʊ/ before the letters *k* and *d* (as in *cooking, look, book, good, stood, wood*). The spelling *ea* normally represents the sound /iy/, though it very often has the sound /ɛ/ before the letters *d, s, th,* and *v* (as in *already, head, bread, pleasant, measure, weather, heavy*). It has the sound /ey/ in only a few words, including *break, great,* and *steak*. As with other vowel spellings, all of these vowel pairs often may have different sounds before *r*.

4 Play the conversation twice. The first time, play it through without stopping. Then replay it, pausing at the ends of sentences to give students time to write in the words from the box.

Answers

A: How was your vacation?
B: Fabulous !
A: You went to Colorado, right?
B: Right.
A: Did a   group   of   you   go?
B: No, just my   cousin   and me.
A: Where did you stay? Did you camp   out ?

B: No, actually, we rented a   house   in Boulder.
A: Wow, it   sounds   great!
B: Yeah. The   country   around there was beautiful.
A: How was the weather?
B: Well, kind of   cloudy   .
A: What did you do there? Did you do any shopping?
B: Oh, I bought some   souvenirs   . And I   found   this   blouse   .
A: It's nice. What else did you do?
B: We went   south   for a few days for some skiing in the   mountains   .
A: I've never gone skiing. It sounds too   dangerous   .
B: Well, I've had a few falls, but nothing too   serious   .
A: Would   you go back?
B: I'd like to. The only   trouble   was, there were too many   tourists   !

6   Answers

1. fabulous, serious, dangerous   (unstressed /ə/)
2. country, trouble, cousin   (/ə/)
3. group, you, souvenirs   (/uw/)
4. house, out, south, blouse, cloudy, sounds, mountains, found   (/aw/)
5. tourists, would   (/ʊ/)

Group 4 shows the most common pronunciation for *ou*: /aw/.

Note that *you* is pronounced as /yuw/ in isolation (group 3) but usually has the weak pronunciation /yə/ or /yu/ in connected speech (the weak form /yə/ is practiced in Unit 46).

You may want to point out additional words in the conversation spelled with *ou* (*your, Boulder, around, bought*) and, perhaps, to ask whether these words fit into the groups listed. Note that some people pronounce *your* as /yʊr/ (Group 5), while other speakers say /yɔr/ (not one of the pronunciations listed); the weak form of *your* has unstressed /ə/. The *ou* stands for the sound /ow/ in *Boulder*, /aw/ in *around* (Group 4), and /ɔ/ in *bought*.

7   During pairwork, monitor the pronunciation of vowel pairs.

Other questions might include: "Do you prefer to rent a house, stay in a hotel, or camp out?"

UNIT 60   Silent letters

1   Answers

ras~~p~~berry   clim~~b~~   ~~k~~nee   i~~s~~land   hal~~f~~
colum~~n~~   ~~k~~now   han~~d~~kerchief   lis~~t~~en   ~~k~~nife
~~h~~our   t~~w~~o   Chris~~t~~mas   ans~~w~~er   veg~~e~~table
com~~b~~   ~~h~~onest   tal~~k~~   han~~d~~some   si~~g~~n
~~p~~sychology   ev~~e~~ry   busi~~n~~ess   ca~~l~~m

Note that some American and Canadian speakers pronounce the *l* in words such as *calm* and *palm*.

2   During repetition, make sure that the letters with the lines through them are not pronounced.

3   Answers

The words with silent letters are listed below:

1. 2   cou<u>l</u>d, wal<u>k</u>
2. 4   <u>h</u>onor, o<u>h</u>, ex<u>h</u>austed, r<u>h</u>ythm
3. 3   dou<u>b</u>t, lam<u>b</u>, bom<u>b</u>
4. 3   forei<u>g</u>n, desi<u>g</u>ner, resi<u>g</u>n
5. 1   We<u>d</u>nesday

You might point out that the second *e* in *Wedn<u>e</u>sday* is also silent.

6   Answers

int~~e~~resting   choc~~o~~late   practic~~a~~lly   gover~~n~~ment   elementar~~y~~
sev~~e~~ral   av~~e~~rage   pos~~t~~card   diff~~e~~rent   fami~~l~~y   fact~~o~~ry
valua~~b~~le   comf~~o~~rtable   aspi~~r~~in   gran~~d~~father   fav~~o~~rite

Note that in the words here in which the silent letter is a vowel (this includes all the words except for *government, postcard,* and *grandfather*), the word is pronounced with one less syllable than it appears to have. For example, *interesting* is said as three syllables and *chocolate* as two syllables.

Other examples of words like the ones in **5** include the following: *sep~~a~~rate, desp~~e~~rate, cam~~e~~ra, temp~~e~~rature, nat~~u~~ral, mis~~e~~rable, us~~u~~ally, accident~~a~~lly, ref~~e~~rence, op~~e~~ra, corp~~o~~rate, trav~~e~~ler,* and *awf~~u~~lly.* Note that the *a* in words ending in -*ically* (like *practic<u>a</u>lly* in **5**) is rarely pronounced.

8 Answers

What's for dessert?	Chocolate cake.
How often do you play softball?	Twice a week on the average.
What's on the news?	The government's raising taxes.
My car was broken into.	Was anything valuable taken?
Do you like this chair?	The other one's more comfortable.
How's your report going?	It's practically finished.
What's your daughter doing?	She just started elementary school.
What do you think of this color?	It's my favorite.
Are these jackets the same?	No, they're different.
Have you ever been to Montreal?	Several times.

You might point out that in the second sentence on the left, the *t* in *often* is usually silent and the *t* in *softball* is often silent in conversation at normal speed.

Monitor the pronunciation of the words shown in **6**, above, during pairwork.

9 Students are to write two-line conversations. The word in the first line of each item should be in the first part of the conversation and the word in the second line should be in the response. When students say the conversations they have written, monitor the pronunciation of the words in the second line.

Answers

The following are some possible conversations:

1. A: What's the book like?
   B: It's really interesting.
2. A: Is there any mail?
   B: Just a postcard from your sister.
3. A: What did you do last weekend?
   B: I visited my family.
4. A: I have a terrible headache.
   B: Have you taken any aspirin?
5. A: Who's the man on the left in the picture?
   B: That's my grandfather when he was young.
6. A: Where do you work?
   B: In a shoe factory.